WOMEN WHO FLY

True Stories by Women Airline Pilots

International Society of Women Airline Pilots

40th Anniversary Commemorative Edition

Women Who Fly
True Stories by Women Airline Pilots

Stories collected by:
Mary Bush Shipko
Kathy McCullough
Bonnie Tiburzi Caputo

These stories are dedicated to our mentors and supporters—
We thank you.

Contents

Flying Stories

Section Two: Friends and Family

SECTION ONE

Flying Stories

Miracle Landing:
Aloha Airlines Flight 243
by Madeline "Mimi" Tompkins

On a balmy, sunny morning in Kailua, Hawaii, I woke to palm trees outside my window and the sound of the ocean on Lanikai Beach. Today was my last day as first officer at Aloha Airlines and I would be flying with one of my favorite captains. It was a luxury to sleep in until 8:00 a.m. because usually I needed to report to work at 4:30 a.m. for the morning shift of inter-island flying.

The following Monday, I would begin training as captain in the Boeing 737-200. This was coming after nine years with Aloha Airlines, minus the four years I was furloughed—or, rather, laid off—because fuel prices were high and people were not traveling as much. I had studied for several months for this upgrade.

With this promotion, I would be the first woman captain for Aloha Airlines, just as I was the first female first officer for the airline in 1979. Several of the (all) male instructors had said they would make sure I didn't pass. I was thirty-six years old and had been flying since my first flight lesson at the age of fourteen. Eight years before being hired at Aloha Airlines, I worked as a flight instructor and flew air cargo in a tail-dragger Beech 18. While furloughed, I also instructed, started my own flight school, purchased a large flight school (Hawaii Country Club of the Air), and worked as a commuter and air ambulance pilot. After flying the 737 for over four years, I had logged over 3500 of my more than 8000 flight hours in that aircraft.

This beautiful day was April 28, 1988, and my flight time for the month was too high so a scheduler offered me the day off. However, I loved my job and looked forward to flying, especially with this crew: Captain Frank Naahielua, First Flight Attendant Clarabelle "CB" Lansing-Ho, Jane Sato-Tomita, and Michelle Honda. They were highly experienced, professional, and most importantly, lots of fun to work with.

After checking in with dispatch and getting a briefing on the weather, pilot NOTAMs (Notice to Airmen), aircraft status, etc., I went out to the aircraft. Charlie Auld, who had flown the first five legs of the morning schedule, greeted me and said that the captain was not Frank. Frank had taken the day off when it was offered by scheduling. Instead I would be flying with a reserve captain, Robert "Bob" Schornstheimer. He was a new captain, forty-two years old, with over 8500 flight hours. He had 6700 hours in Boeing 737s, with about nine months of experience serving as captain on that aircraft. Bob and I had flown together once before. He was a meticulous pilot, highly intelligent, with a great sense of humor. It was going to be a great day!

April in Hawaii is stunning and Maui is especially enchanting. Haleakala, meaning "the house of the sun," sits on the east side of the Kahului Airport (OGG) at 10,023 feet above sea level, and the West Maui mountains, including Pu'u Kukui, the highest peak at 5,788 feet, sits to the west. The airport is in the valley-like isthmus between these peaks.

The air was clear on the flight into Kahului with normal trade winds, which are usually from the northeast at ten to fifteen knots due to a high pressure area that sits about 700 miles northeast of the islands. Normally the final approach into runway 02 is bumpy because the wind is gusty and the wind speed increases from the Venturi effect of mountains on each side of the airport. Our flight was normal and Bob was easy to fly with. He was known to follow standard operating procedures, which makes a first officer's job much easier.

We did a quick turnaround after unloading and loading passengers and then we were on our way to Hilo, on the big island of Hawaii. There was a little light turbulence along the Hamakua coast into Hilo Airport (ITO) but nothing unusual. The view of the rocky coastline and Mauna Kea to the south of us was breathtaking. I never got tired of the scenery flying inter-island. Each crew would fly an average of eight flights per day between the islands. As the sun moves around the sky, the colors change. Often there are rainbows near the "liquid sunshine" of light rain showers in the microclimates of the island valleys and ridges.

The landing in Hilo was uneventful. We had a short break there, and I took lunch orders from the crew. I "radioed" the order in to the Hilo Station personnel who relayed it to the airport restaurant. The Hilo restaurant was famous for good home-cooked local dishes like Portuguese bean soup and loco moko. In celebration of my last flight as first officer, I brought blueberry cheesecake muffins for dessert from a special bakery in Kailua. The crew ate dessert first while I left to pick up their orders.

As I walked down the metal stairs brought up to the aircraft by maintenance, I looked over the tires, then the lower part and side of the fuselage, out of habit. I didn't notice anything amiss. When I returned to the aircraft, I looked at the tires, landing gear, leading edge of the wing, elevator, rudder, and upper fuselage. Again, I did not see anything out of the ordinary. I walked up the outside stairs into the jetway. As I entered the doorway to the aircraft, I didn't notice anything unusual about the doorway structure either.

Cleaning up before the passengers were boarded, Clarabelle Ho-Lansing, or "CB" as we called her, pulled me aside and said she thought I would be a good captain. She said she knew that a lot of the old-timers didn't want a woman captain, but she encouraged me to stay positive and not let them hold me back. This support meant a lot to me.

CB was not one to compliment easily. She was known for her "Pan Am style" professionalism and had worked for Aloha Airlines for thirty-seven years. Every day her uniform was perfect, her long hair swept up in the Hawaiian style with fresh plumeria blossoms on the side. She always carried a baggie of more plumeria flowers so she could keep those in her hair fresh. Her passengers loved her and she gave special attention to children. She usually didn't eat sweets. But that day I talked her into a cheesecake muffin. We ate our dessert together and then quickly got back to work.

As I got back into my copilot's seat for pre-departure checklists, a Hilo agent escorted a jumpseater onto the flight deck. A Hilo Airport air traffic control tower operator was riding with us on an observation flight. Periodically, ATC personnel were required to do this to get a different perspective on their work. The person riding with us told us he did not like to fly and was uncomfortable. Captain Bob, an ex-Air Force pilot/instructor who had also worked as an air traffic controller, immediately put our jumpseater at ease.

It was my leg at the controls for the flight back to Honolulu. Before we taxied out, Bob briefed the control tower operator on the use of the oxygen mask and how to use and stow his seat behind the center console. He discussed our ATC flight clearance, the weather, and other details of the flight to make sure there were no surprises en route.

Bob also mentioned the light turbulence we expected on the departure climb and said it would last until we were some distance from the mountains. There would possibly be a little more turbulence just south of Maui. The flight would only be about forty minutes, and the time would pass quickly. Scenery en route would be varied and interesting. The controller was given a headset so he could listen to the ATC conversations and we also kept the overhead speaker turned on.

The flight departed Hilo at 1:25 p.m. with the regular five crewmembers, the jumpseater on the flight deck, and eighty-nine passengers, bound for Honolulu. There were no unusual occurrences during the take-off and ascent.

Around 1:48 p.m., as the aircraft passed through about 23,500 feet, approximately twenty-six nautical miles (43 km) south-southeast of Kahului, Maui, I felt a small jerk in the rudder petals and an unusual feeling in the fuselage that could have been turbulence. I turned to Bob to ask if he felt it and saw he was talking to the controller. I didn't have time to interrupt him or even get my sentence out when it felt like someone had kicked me in the chest. All the air was instantly out of my lungs. I saw a gray mist that quickly cleared, my contact lenses lifted on my eyes, and I closed my eyes for a second, then opened them with contacts intact. It felt like something had hit the left side of the aircraft as the aircraft yawed and rolled left and right several times.

I lost several seconds. I had just started the level off and remember seeing the altitude around 23,900 feet. Then I saw the altimeter at 23,400 feet and descending. It was like a bad dream. I tried to wake up and couldn't. I thought for a second that I was in a simulator checkride because so many overhead lights were on. There was a piece of fiberglass plastered on my altitude indicator on the instrument panel. It looked like a feather. Grey insulation was flying around the flight deck. I thought, "Maybe we hit a bird." I glanced back and saw the flight deck door was gone and I could see sky and an opening on the left side of the cabin. Again, my mind tried to make sense of what was happening. "Maybe the cargo door opened," I thought, even though we were not in a cargo aircraft.

Meanwhile, my original flight instructor, Walter Shell, from southeast Texas, became a voice in my head calmly saying, "Fly the airplane. Fly the airplane. Fly until the noise stops." This had been his mantra for our emergency training exercises. I reached over to reduce the power for an emergency descent and saw that Bob had lost his headset and his sunglasses were at an odd position on his head. My own headset and sunglasses were gone.

I did not know the extent of the damage. A small section on the left side of the roof had ruptured initially, then the upper fuselage quickly ripped backwards. The resulting very rapid decompression was so violent that the cockpit door was blown off its hinges, part of the cabin floor was lifted upwards, and eighteen feet of the upper fuselage was torn away, all in a split second. This large section of the roof consisted of the entire top half of the aircraft skin extending from just behind the cockpit to the fore-wing area.

Bob later said that, when he looked back, he could see blue sky, jagged metal aft of where the top had ripped off, and bloodied faces on the passengers who were swaying sideways in their seats as the aircraft yawed. I too could see two of the front passengers who appeared to be injured and bloody.

What mattered was that the aircraft was still flying, responding to input, and we had to descend so passengers could breathe. After he put on his oxygen mask, Bob signaled me with hand motions and eye contact that he was taking over control of the aircraft. I nodded and released the control wheel when I felt his positive control. Immediately I put on my mask and we initiated the emergency descent checklist after realizing that the loss of pressurization checklist could not help. We had oxygen but were not sure if the cabin oxygen system was working, so it was extremely important to quickly get down to a lower altitude where there was enough oxygen in the outside air to support life.

One of the Aloha flight instructors had recommended that I memorize all the critical checklists instead of just those that were required. I had done this for upgrade training, so my confidence in knowing what to do without a physical checklist could not have been higher. Bob flew the aircraft as we descended at a high rate in idle, at the airspeed the incident occurred, which is what to do when structural damage is suspected, as per our checklist. For us, that was the 280 to 290 knots at which we had been when leveling off. As I completed the checklists, I set the emergency code 7700 on the transponder, which indicated to radar Air Traffic Control that we had an emergency. I tried to call ATC but got no answer. Bob looked at me to see if I had contacted anyone. He used a hand signal to me that we would proceed to Maui because the noise in the cockpit was as loud as standing right next to a train. I could hear nothing but the roar. We had to communicate with hand signals, pointing to gauges and switches.

I noticed that Bob's headset was not over his ears and realized I wouldn't get an answer from ATC because my headset was missing. I found mine on the floor next to my seat and was barely able to hear. I called Maui Approach Control. There was some confusion because we were not scheduled to stop in Maui on this flight and there was also another Aloha flight near Maui with a similar call sign.

At 10,000 feet we leveled briefly and I realized the left engine was not working. Besides this problem, Bob said later it felt like we were in manual reversion, which means a loss of all hydraulics, including no "boost" on the aircraft flight controls. He pointed to the gauge that showed we still had all our hydraulics. It felt confusing because of how much effort he had to use to keep the aircraft flying in the direction he wanted.

I tried to call the flight attendants and turned to see if I could contact CB. I knew she would come into the cockpit if she were able. I tried several times to call Michelle who was working in the back of the aircraft. No answer.

Bob turned towards Maui about twenty miles out, when we were clear of the Haleakala dormant volcano. There were scattered clouds and Bob steered around them.

In the Air Force, Bob had learned and taught pilots to do controllability checks when an aircraft may have had structural damage. He turned the aircraft left and right in gentle banks, then decided to slow and configure for landing earlier than usual so that he could test for minimum controllable speed to land.

We were on a long, high, visual approach to runway 02 when we extended the flaps from 5 to 15 degrees. The aircraft quickly reacted by buffeting—not a good sign. The pitch of the aircraft was more nose down than at flaps 5, and the airflow in the cockpit changed significantly. Immediately I asked Bob, "Is it better with flaps up?" He reached for the flap lever, too, and said, "Put 'em back to 5." With the flaps back at 5 degrees the buffeting went away.

At about seven or eight miles from the runway and off to the left side of final approach, we did not know that there were pieces of fuselage stuck in the leading edge devices on one side. As Bob flew, the control wheel was moving much more than usual left and right. This was the only time I thought we would not make it to the runway. I started looking around for a place to land the aircraft and a found a sugar cane field with a road I thought we could possibly land on. Remembering my thoughts later, I realized it was a field suitable for a general aviation aircraft, but it would not have worked well for a Boeing 737.

Everyone asks if I was afraid. I only remember feeling calm. At times it seemed quiet and not quite real. Time was distorted. Sometimes things seemed to happen in slow motion; however, at other times, time was racing and I didn't think we could get to everything we needed to do in time for landing. A couple of times, when I was not touching a switch or handle, I would "see" Bob and I flying the aircraft from the back of the cockpit. I focused on watching Bob so that I could assist him in any way I could.

The nose landing gear indicator, which normally shines green to show that the gear is locked down, was not glowing. At this point, though, we were in contact with Maui Tower. Bob reached over and tapped on the light to test it. I did the same, but it did not work. Bob said, "Pull the manual handle." I had to tap on the shoes of the jumpseater to get him to move his feet so I could access the handles. He was huddled between and behind us trying to avoid getting hit with small objects that were flying into the flight deck area. I manually pulled all three landing gear release handles.

I told Maui Tower that we were landing without a nose gear. At this point, the nose gear seemed like a minor problem because we had to land no matter what. Bob was using approximately normal takeoff thrust on our one "good" engine to maintain the glide path to the runway, and there was no possibility of leveling off or going around. We had to approach faster than 170 knots because the aircraft reacted badly when we tried to fly slower.

Bob made a perfect landing! He greased it on. While we were rolling down the runway, I put out full flaps to help us stop. The nose gear touched and we both started to breathe. Bob stopped the aircraft short of runway 05, so that there would still be one usable runway at the airport. We faced the jumpseater who could not figure out how to get the jump seat up so that he could get out of the cockpit doorway. Bob was telling him how to do it, and I was yelling, "Jump over it!" and the Maui air traffic controller was calling to us over the radio: "Shut down the engine!"

We then realized the engine was running, looked at each other, and went through the Emergency Evacuation checklist. I couldn't remember any items on this checklist, so I looked around and found the checklist book on the floor. I read the checklist, and Bob completed all the items.

I felt tremendous relief for just a few seconds. We each went back to the cabin and I couldn't make sense of what I was looking at. The forward part of the cabin aisle floor had lifted upwards and was now over my head. I couldn't look down the aisle.

I saw a woman jump onto the emergency slide on the left side of the aircraft. The slide deflated and she landed on both feet then fell face forward on the pavement and didn't move. Her husband started to jump and I held him back. He kept slipping out of my hands because he was covered in blood. I yelled at someone at the base of the slide to hold the bottom of the slide away from the airplane to support it. He did so just as the man jumped to be with his wife. He looked like he was okay.

Bob and I heard a strange noise that turned out to be the tires deflating, as they are designed to do so when heavy braking is used during emergencies to prevent them from exploding from overheating. I still could not hear well. In fact, for me, there was total silence for many minutes after we landed.

I climbed over the seats to get to the back. I saw passengers standing and getting their bags from the overhead bins as if it was a normal de-boarding. I approached a tall passenger who had blood running down the side of his face. I asked him to turn around and go to the back exit to get off the aircraft. He smiled at me and said, "I'm one of the lucky ones. I'm not hurt." Then he turned around to work his way to the back. I found out later that this person was someone I had known for many years. At the time I did not recognize him.

I saw Second Fight Attendant Michelle Honda helping passengers towards the back of the plane. She was working her way up the aisle towards Bob and me. We did not see Flight Attendant CB Lansing-Ho. Michelle reached the front where we were helping with passengers and asked Bob if I could assist her getting the passengers off the plane. He agreed. Bob climbed down a fireman's ladder to make sure there were no problems on the ground and to check on passengers.

Michelle was unbelievably brave. She had been sucked off her feet by the rapid depressurization. As she gained awareness, she used deep breathing to stabilize and calm herself enough to continue her duties. She, too, was able to remember her emergency checklists and assisted passengers in putting on their life vests. Michelle believed we would ditch until she felt us level off slightly and turn towards Maui Airport. At that point she knew Bob and I were okay.

During the flight, Michelle had even crawled up the aisle into the open area where the cabin roof was missing and tried to pull Jane Sato-Tomita to safety. She was unable to move Jane and got one of the passengers next to her to hold onto her. Passengers on the aisle held Michelle down as she crawled up and back down the aisle, instructing them to put on their life vests and assist in any way she could.

After landing, two nurses from Hilo who initially had been told to evacuate the aircraft with other passengers came back on the aircraft to help with the injured. Several passengers were unable to get up and walk, and many others needed medical assistance. Some passengers were also helping each other. A frequent flyer gave up his shirt to be used for bandages and assisted the nurses in performing triage.

After everyone was off the plane, I picked up our flight bags and any personal items I could find on the flight deck. When all passengers were accounted for, and those needing medical assistance were receiving it, Bob and I walked around the plane to check the damage. That's when Michelle came up and told us that CB was missing. Bob immediately requested a Coast Guard search to be initiated for CB near where the cabin top had come off.

We found out later that CB had been instantly killed when she was sucked out of the aircraft during the rapid depressurization. Jane, who was standing next to her hit the ceiling, fell back down, and was tangled in the area where the floor ripped up in the forward cabin area.

The aftermath of the flight was more difficult for me than the flight.

I was prepared for inflight emergencies. Bob was an excellent pilot. I never once doubted his ability to get us on the ground and I did my best to assist him. However, when I studied and visualized flight emergencies before Flight 243, I never imagined what would happen after I was on the ground other than knowing that I was supposed to grab my hat, get off, and try to keep passengers together and away from the aircraft. I assumed other people would take over and handle the rescue. I didn't realize how long it takes them to get rescue crews to the aircraft and how much we as crewmembers do before they arrive.

Bob, Michelle, and I ended up in a command center at the Maui Police station where compassionate officers and staff cared for us by providing phones so we could make calls to company personnel and others. Then we were asked to return to the airport to talk with an FBI agent and FAA representatives. Local Air Line Pilots Association Safety Committee members arrived to assist and support us, and Bob spoke on the phone with an ALPA Accident Investigation team member in Herndon, Virginia.

We were in Maui all afternoon and evening until the runway was reopened so that another 737 could land and take us and the passengers back to Honolulu. Smaller island airplanes had been able to land earlier and bring supplies for the hospital as well as company personnel, investigators, etc. Several passengers stayed at the hospital in Maui when we departed, as did Flight Attendant Jane Sato-Tomita.

That night, for me, was spent at a hotel. News media were surrounding Bob's home and were near the apartment I rented. We each spent a few days at a North Shore hotel until our National Transportation Safety Board (NTSB) interview was completed.

Bob and I both were eager to go back to work. I wanted to join my upgrade class for training, but this was delayed a few weeks. I did eventually complete this training. However, it wasn't until the following August that I first flew as captain. After that, I went on to work for Aloha Airlines for another twenty years. I also poured my energy into helping develop a Critical Incident Response Program for airline crewmembers and employees.

I learned many lessons from this accident. First, a pilot cannot be overly prepared. Technical proficiency, knowledge of systems, checklists, and operating procedures are all critical. Second, teamwork is vital to safety and this includes Crew Resource Management (CRM) skills. Those skills had not yet been taught at Aloha Airlines, but Captain Schornstheimer naturally had high situational awareness and excellent decision-making, workload management, and communication skills, all the core principles of CRM. Third, flight attendants can save your life! Listen to them. They are highly trained safety professionals. Fourth, I gained immense respect for the Boeing 737 aircraft. Ours took incredible abuse as it came apart, and despite the damage, it got us home.

And last but most important, when you are offered a day off by scheduling, take it!

Madeline "Mimi" Tompkins was hired by Aloha Airlines in 1979. She flew Boeing 737s for 29 years in Hawaii, the South Pacific, and US and Canada's west coast. Aloha went out of business in 2008 and she went to work for Hawaiian Airlines flying the Boeing 717 and 767. Mimi has retired and lives with her husband, Captain Bill Morin (Alaska Airlines) in Hawaii and Washington State.

Aloha Airlines Boeing 737-297 - Photo credit: Wikipedia

From Russia With Love:
Emergency Landing in Petropavlosk
by Glenys Robison

"We have a trip for you tomorrow, skipper, a three-dayer to Shanghai, are you interested?" After twenty-five years of domestic flying I had finally made it to my dream job—flying around the world left seat on a Boeing 767, and this call from crew scheduling had me stoked. I'd never been to Shanghai but my sister had lived there in the 1980s, so I was thrilled to be going to a place that she loved.

This would be my third trip as a B767 captain and I needed to prepare. I pulled out books and charts and spent a few hours reviewing the route, alternates, weather forecasts, and company briefing notes on Russian and Chinese airspace. The next morning I arrived at the airport very early to print weather charts and NOTAMs and to talk to the company dispatcher who planned the flight. There are often active volcanoes in Russia and I was concerned about one that was rumbling near our route.

It was a beautiful day that started without a hitch. My crew consisted of a first officer and cruise relief pilot (RP). The first officer was another woman pilot that I'd flown with early in her career, and I knew her to be a very competent and keen pilot. The junior crew member—the relief pilot—was new to me, but I learned he'd been in the Canadian Air Force flying CF-18s and now, with the airline, he frequently flew the route we were on. I was happy to have such a great crew as we worked our way westward, passing from Vancouver to Anchorage ATC and on to the more demanding Russian airspace.

With the first officer on her break in the back and the relief pilot and I chatting about what we expected ahead, a call came from the In-Charge flight attendant. "I have some bad news," he said. "All of the aft lavatories have quit." While we were going through some reset procedures in the flight deck and trying to get a patch through to our company maintenance, the In-Charge called again to say he had some really bad news—all of the lavs in the aircraft had quit. Losing four lavs on a long flight would be challenging but losing all eight lavs could quickly become a crisis. We began to consider our options. Anchorage was 2000 miles behind us, Japan 1500 ahead, and Shanghai was another 1000 miles beyond that. No matter which way we turned, we had several hours before we could find a suitable landing spot.

While talking with the company on a high frequency radio patch, we got our third call from the back. The In-Charge now reported that a passenger said there was smoke coming from the mid-lavatory. The RP leapt out of his seat and returned in seconds. "It's bad," he said. "It stinks of electrical smoke."

A pilot's worst nightmare—fire on board. There are pages and pages of procedures to follow when you have unidentified smoke or fire on board, but there are only two words that you need to remember when you start your drills: Land ASAP. The RP declared an emergency as we turned off the airway and began to descend. The Russian town of Petropavlosk was 120 miles northwest of our position and we made a beeline direct. The first officer returned to take her seat and began to program our arrival into the FMS.

It's understandable that a Mayday call, smoke, and diversion into Russia would arouse the company managers from their summer slumbers. No flight had ever diverted to Russia in the company's history, and managers and emergency responders from all departments were brought together in a crisis room in Montreal, preparing for any outcome.

Meanwhile, we did everything we could to secure the flight. There was no evidence of continuing fire, and other than the lavs, all systems appeared to be operating normally. We briefed for the approach and drifted down to Petro.

Having retold this story a number of times, I learned that some pilots' second worst nightmare is a diversion to a Russian airport. They do things differently there. Radio transmissions are often poor and hard to understand in thick Russian accents. Measures such as speeds and winds are in metric, and minimum altitudes are referenced to meters above ground level while most other countries use feet above sea level. Thankfully the winds favored the only useable approach and the sky was clear, so our calculations were kept to a minimum.

Radio transmissions were amazingly short. I recall only two: "Cleared for the approach" and "Cleared to land." The brevity belied the tension that was building around us. We were descending to land at the largest nuclear submarine base in the world, and Russian authorities were no doubt on high alert with our unannounced arrival. We landed to a smattering of applause from our relieved passengers and worked our way slowly towards the ramp. We passed camouflaged bunkers with netted roofs, their hardware hidden from prying eyes, and an impressive assortment of old and new military and civilian aircraft. We were motioned to park on an empty pad south of the tiny terminal building. It was a bit surreal as the ground handler gave us hand signals to taxi right up to a short chain-link fence. Our nose was almost over a kid's park. I could see two girls gleefully pounding up and down on a see-saw.

We shut down the engines, unlocked the doors, and waited. And waited some more. Someone pushed airstairs up to the door and entered. They wanted a report and informed us that no one could leave the airplane. We needed maintenance, lavatory service, flight planning, fuel, and a way to contact our company. They left, promising to return. Nothing at all happened for what seemed like a very long time.

Finally the airport staff jumped to attention when a long black shiny limousine pulled up to the fence. The gates opened, the limo passed through and stopped nearby. The back door was opened and out stepped the most dashing figure imaginable. He was tall and lean and freshly shaved in a beautiful suit, fedora, pink silk tie with matching breast handkerchief, and impossibly long lizard-skin cowboy boots that were slightly curled at the ends. The Petropavlosk Director General was briefed and I could see his final nod. Da, we could have service.

Another hour passed. We had an intermittent satellite line to company headquarters and tried to plan a departure. If our crew duty time was kept short and the aircraft was service-able, we would plan to Tokyo, but if the delay persisted, we would plan to Anchorage. If the day was stretched further, there weren't many options. One hotel in town had 50 rooms.

Sleeping on board the aircraft until a recovery airplane could be brought to Petropavlosk would be our last resort.

Again the fence gate opened. This time a stocky man in a red T-shirt and camouflaged pants approached, cigarette in hand, followed by a raggedy dog that plopped down under the nose wheel to await his master's return. Our mechanic came up and this was when we learned that our In-Charge spoke fluent Russian! The two of them went to inspect the lavs, open panels, and troubleshoot our problem. Things were starting to click. Lavatory and fuel trucks arrived, and someone brought a flight plan for Tokyo, showing Shanghai as the alternate, so we could make further decisions once airborne.

The most wonderful woman came aboard, too. She asked me to sign twelve pages of incomprehensible Russian text. Similarly, we asked the mechanic to sign eight pages of incomprehensible English text. She briefed me on the departure, weather, and the next four assigned radio frequencies, and finally informed me that I would not be "personally responsible" for any charges incurred that day. A massive tug was attached to the nose wheel. We received our clearance: "You are cleared to destination." Two more transmissions came from the controller: "Cleared to taxi" was followed by "Cleared for take-off." That's it, that's all we ever heard from him.

As we lifted off and turned westward into the setting sun, I could see the massive snow-covered volcanoes that ring the city and the deep-water harbor shadowed by steep cliffs. Lights twinkled below and ahead lay utter emptiness. I promised that someday I would return to explore this beautiful part of the world. It wasn't scary at all.

Glenys enjoyed a thirty-four-year career with Air Canada as a pilot, flight manager, and chief pilot. Retired on the Boeing 767 in 2013, Captain Robison lives with her life partner of twenty-eight years in British Columbia.

Highlights
by Emily Howell Warner

After high school, I took a commercial flight and was the only passenger on the airplane. Right after we took off, I asked one of the flight attendants, "Do you think I could go up and see the cockpit?" She said, "Sure, I think so. I'll see if they'll let you come up." The pilots opened the door and I looked out the front window and thought, *This is neat.* The copilot said, and I will never forget this…, "If you think you like flying, you should take lessons." I asked, "Can a girl take flying lessons?" He said, "Sure." He told me to go to Clinton Aviation. His words changed my life.

I started taking flying lessons. My mother noticed and kept telling me, "I don't know about this Emily, I think it's kind of foolish." I would respond, "Oh, just a couple more, Mother, just a couple more." That was how I convinced her to let me continue. One day I came home and told my mother that I had soloed the airplane. She said, "You mean you went by yourself?" I nodded. She thought about it for a minute and said, "Well, I guess that's okay. Maybe these flying lessons are okay."

I just couldn't believe it. Eventually, when I was a flight instructor, I took my parents up for a flight. My mother asked, "Can I try it?" I said, "Sure, just handle the controls real easy." And she did.

When I was a copilot at Frontier Airlines, I flew with some nice people, but I knew I would eventually have to fly with one senior captain who had a reputation. When we got on the airplane he said, "Don't touch anything." He flew the whole flight and I just sat there. It was a very quiet flight. At the end of the trip I told him, "I really enjoyed flying with you."

A few months later I flew with the number two captain at Frontier. We flew a whole month together, and everyone really respected him. At the end of the month he said, "Well Emily, you're just one of the fellas now." Word got around, and because everyone liked him so much, I was accepted.

I only had one engine failure in my whole career. The engine failed while I was flying and I did what I was supposed to do. Then I said, "Captain, do you want to take it over?" He said, "No, you're doing fine. Just keep flying it and I'll take care of the radios and everything else." About that time the cockpit door flew open. A couple of flight attendants came in and asked in panicky voices, "What's wrong? What's wrong?" The captain was cool and collected. I could see why he wanted me to fly. That way he could handle the rest. He said to them, "We've had an engine failure and everything is fine. We're going to be landing soon. I'm going to make an announcement." Then he added, "Please don't barge into the cockpit again."

He let me land the plane at our destination. When we got on the ground, I was so excited. He said, "Let's go walk around the airplane and see what happened." As we walked around the plane, he said to me, "You look like you're happy about this." I said, "I am! It's my first engine failure!"

Emily was hired by Frontier Airlines in 1973 as a first officer on the Twin Otter. After working as an FAA Designated Pilot Examiner, Captain Warner retired in the early 1990s and is living in Colorado.

Emily poses with her sketch at the Aviation Hall of Fame.

Bad Luck Comes in Threes
by Liz Jennings Clark

I was a relatively young first officer with LIAT (Leeward Islands Air Transport), an island-hopping airline with propeller aircraft in the Caribbean. The year was 1986. I'd been with them three years. It was my first job after flying school and I was their first female pilot. I started on the Embraer Bandeirante; that was sold and I moved to the DHC Twin Otter and flew about 1300 hours on that. Then I was fresh out of training for the—then new—De Havilland Dash 8 (100 series). We were not the launch customer but number two or three, and I believe the aircraft I was called out to fly was number thirteen from the factory production line.

Being called from standby in Antigua was slightly unusual. It was really hard to get a telephone line installed on this small island without making an exorbitant payment to someone at the phone company. Mobile phones were only on Star Trek, so the solution was a van driver who came along to your apartment and knocked on the door for as long as it took to wake you…along with a few of your neighbors who, in my case, were LIAT cabin crew, so at least they understood the situation!

At 5 a.m. on a rainy, stormy morning, I was told that I was needed for the route up through St. Maarten, Beef Island, St. Thomas, and St. Croix, returning that same way to Antigua. Eight stretches was a pretty long day of flying. We were with a Canadian De Havilland captain who was with us until we got enough route exposure on the brand-new aircraft. I had flown with him before and was happy he was the commander. He let you do your stuff but also gave tips and shared his vast experience in a constructive manner.

We did the first-flight-of-the-day checks upon arrival at the airport—a somewhat extended checklist since the aircraft had stood overnight. The cabin crew loaded the simple catering, and we boarded an almost full load of passengers. During taxi out, we got a warning light for the right-hand electronic engine control unit. It was not functioning. That was a "no go" item. We turned around and headed back to the platform to let the engineers have a look. Their suggestion was to take the other new Dash 8 that was parked up on the platform while they figured out the issues on this one. So off we went for a second time. First flight checks and catering were done and passengers were boarded, so we started engines, taxied out, and…oh, no! The left-hand electronic engine control unit was unserviceable. What were the odds?!

So, back to the ramp. The tech guys figured the quickest solution was to remove the right-hand EEC from the first aircraft, install it in the left-hand engine of the second, and we should be good to go. This time we did an engine run-up before we asked for the passengers to re-embark.

Off we went. We got airborne and climbed out quite quickly with our light load and commented on the clearing skies. After a weekend of heavy tropical rain, the atmosphere was washed clean. The Canadian captain asked me to confirm which islands he was looking at, as some of the smaller ones were not on our route network. We were glad to finally be on our way.

The captain was flying and I was working the radios. We were climbing out of 20,000 feet when we were switched over to San Juan radar—the Puerto Rico Air Traffic Control station has responsibility for a wide area of upper airspace. I started to make our initial contact report when a loud noise made me jump. It was as though a gun had been fired in the cockpit. I was looking down at the instruments to check our passing altitude as the bang happened. When I looked up, I saw that my window had shattered. There were hundreds of cracks, looking like crazy paving. The captain reached across to check that I still had my shoulder harness on.

A switch flicked.

We were in an emergency situation. At any moment the whole windscreen could give way. I informed San Juan we would be performing an emergency descent. We were very glad that there was a hole in the clouds—this was long before there was a traffic collision avoidance system, so it was basically "see and avoid." We didn't know how long the window could hold, and we were almost at the maximum operating altitude. A decompression would not have been pretty.

We got down to 10,000 feet, caught our breath, and told Antigua operations we were heading back for the third time that morning. The captain asked if there was another crew who could be called out so that we could be released. They answered, "Sorry, but you guys were the standby crew!"

After landing in Antigua, we walked across to the second Dash 8 and started the whole thing again. Eight stretches but now with only seven passengers, as many had decided not to fly that day by that time. In retrospect, I was glad to be getting back on a horse after it had bolted. We went off again, and this time we completed a normal day's work.

When I got home, I realized that, as is common in a small island, news travels fast. A bunch of pilots and cabin crew were waiting for me in the apartment I shared with a stewardess. They were deep into a rum and coke fueled discussion as to whether I would have been sucked out of the plane or if the airspeed would have caused the glass to fly in and cut my face....

Liz was hired in 1983 by the Caribbean airline, LIAT. Captain Jennings Clark is now flying the Boeing 737 for Transavia Airlines—a Dutch airline based in Amsterdam. Liz was born in the UK, grew up in St. Lucia with Irish roots, and … "enjoys the photos life presents."

In a Place Called the Cockpit
by Bonnie Tiburzi Caputo

t was just another night flight and not much more than an air taxi ride from La Guardia Airport to Buffalo, New York. The sort of bid you draw when you're a young flight officer with only a few weeks on the line and very little seniority. Matter-of-fact, I was the most junior crew member on the entire American Airlines seniority roster.

Thunderstorms had threatened all day, but so far the weather had held in a glowering sort of way. In the darkness of the leaden summer night, I did my preflight check. The only slight irregularity was that one generator bore a placard reading INOPERATIVE. But that presented no problem. It had no effect on the operation of the three engines of the Boeing 727, all of which were running flawlessly. All I would have to do would be to reduce some of the less vital electrical functions, such as galley power when not needed and the fans used to draw air into the plane during takeoff while the flaps are down.

We taxied out onto the runway and lifted off into the murk, Captain Roger Norton in the left seat, copilot Larry Fuller on his right and me—I was at the flight engineer's desk behind them. The flaps came up, the pressure controls were set, and my after-takeoff checklist was complete.

Everything was normal, even if a little bumpy, as we cruised at 20,000 feet. The number one flight attendant, Jessie Knowles, sat in the cockpit talking to us, her preliminary duties taken care of and everything in the cabin under control. In a moment we would be climbing sedately through 24,000 feet on the way to our final cruising altitude.

I glanced at my panel again, automatically double-checking the compact array of lights and gauges. Fuel tanks 1 and 3 were turned off, fuel tank 2 was on, and the cabin was maintaining the correct air pressure. I had set the cabin altitude to climb at 500 feet per minute, much more slowly than the aircraft's rate of climb, so that at a height of 24,000 feet the cabin pressure would correspond to a comfortable altitude of no more than 1,000 to 1,500 feet. Outside, the sky was heavy with unspent rain. Cumulonimbus clouds floated around us. The air was unstable, perhaps turbulent enough to compel some attention from nervous passengers but nothing to cause alarm. Just some little potholes in the sky.

Then, with heart-stopping suddenness there was a sucking of air through the cockpit. My ears popped. Blood pounded in my head and everything went black for one split second. Swift, simultaneous actions appeared as if on slow-motion film, playing out in stately, measured steps—reflex movements that, in fact, took only a flash of time.

With the first rush of air I knew the cabin pressure had plummeted. It was as if the plane had become a balloon, losing its air in one whooshing gust. Still, in that first instant, as I reached for my oxygen mask and looked at my pressure controls, I saw that the cabin altitude was shooting up at a rate of two thousand feet a minute. I pulled on my mask and turned to the flight attendant to tell her, but she was already up and out, in one instinctive swift movement to be with the passengers. Admiration flooded one part of my mind as another part realized that the captain had leveled off at twenty thousand feet, preparing to descend if necessary, wisely not making any drastic moves.

I reached automatically for the toggle switch marked PASSENGER OXYGEN. But I stopped. I had a sudden memory of being in the training simulator: the same darkness of the cockpit broken by the glimmering gold and silver instruments and, outside, the silhouette of clouds against the moonlight, a lurching loss of pressure, and a voice reminding me, "Don't pull that switch too soon. You don't know that you need it. Wait. Evaluate."

I left the switch untouched, thinking of that great orange grove of oxygen masks dropping down and enveloping the passengers. There's no need to scare them—not yet. Don't do anything to aggravate a situation we haven't defined.

Intently, I worked with the pressurization controls on my panel. What we had was a rapid depressurization. What we didn't have was a reason for it. When I adjust my pressurization controls as we climb, outflow valves open and shut to suck out little quantities of air. When the cabin suddenly starts to climb at two thousand feet per minute, the indication is that the air is being sucked out in one enormous gulp. One of two things can be wrong: there's a nasty hole in the plane and within seconds we're going to have an explosive decompression as part of the cargo compartment falls out, in which case we have to get down fast before everybody turns blue, or else there's an outflow valve stuck wide open, sucking all the air out.

But there was nothing on my panel to pinpoint the problem. There was nothing even indicating any problem. The panel lights, small gleams of amber, showed normal configuration.

I heard the muffled voice of Captain Norton talking through his oxygen mask to the copilot. "Turn around and help her," he said. Larry turned, an oddly clumsy figure in his mask, saw the lights glowing on my panel and made an automatic gesture with his hand.

Just as automatically, I said, "Would you please turn around and do your job?"

And like a diver deep under water, he turned clumsily away. There was no need for his help at my desk and he knew it.

My ears pounded and the adrenaline pumped as we skimmed through the dark. I wondered whether we had blown a hole somewhere on the fuselage. One of us—me—would have to go back and check it out.

The cabin altitude was climbing. Five thousand feet...six thousand feet. I was conscious of being in a very small world of panels and controls, as beloved and familiar as the dashboard of my first car, locked in by silvery darkness and the capricious currents of air. We became one with the machine.

There was a change on my panel. The cabin altitude was slowing, reversing, steadying, coming back to normal. There was no big bang, no dramatic resolution. Whatever had happened was over. It might only have been a sticky outflow value after all.

The captain pushed the throttles forward. The nose of the aircraft pointed up and we started to climb. Masks off, we looked human again. Larry half-turned toward me and gave a faint grin. He seemed relieved. So was I, but why that particular look at me?

But then I had time to think, and the answer dawned on me. The captain had been a little apprehensive of me, probably thinking, "Omigod, the girl's done something wrong! Help her!!"

Damn them. But maybe I shouldn't blame them for being unsure of me. Not only was I new to the job, but I was also the first woman they had flown with. For the first and almost the last time, I was aware that my being a woman in the cockpit, that bastion of masculinity, was more of a problem for the men than it was for me. I was used to male fliers. But they weren't used to me.

Airline flying was traditionally a macho job, sought after by the guys with the right stuff and a particular kind of cool swagger. Those attributes may be reassuring, but coordination, training, and a fierce desire to do the job as well as it can be done are far more important than male muscles.

Perhaps if I had been bigger it might have been easier for all of us. Picture this: I am 5 feet, 6 1/4 inches tall, weigh in at 125 pounds, and am distinctly lacking in bulging biceps. I play tennis, love to ski, and I jog. My dark hair hangs down almost to my shoulders because I like it that way. I wear a white blouse with an ascot and a designer uniform cap. Both handpicked by me.

When I started flying out of Buffalo in 1973, I was an unsophisticated twenty-four-year-old who was only peripherally conscious of what it might mean to be the first woman to join the flight crew of a major airline and the first woman on the planet to become a flight engineer on a turbojet aircraft. In small ways it was apparent that the men didn't know how to treat me. Were they supposed to open doors for me and carry my bags? Should they compliment me on the cut of my uniform or pretend they didn't notice? Was I going to be their kid sister or a stiff-necked prude getting uptight about their sexist jokes? Does one pilot ask another pilot for a date?

And now bigger questions had come up. Would I panic in a crisis? Did I really know my job?

I hoped they knew the answers now. After that one instant when I'd said indignantly that I would do my own work, the two men had left me to it, and we had become a smoothly functioning team. Something had happened. It was *our* world up there. We knew what we were there for, and nothing else existed for us but to fly the airplane. So one flight crew member wore lipstick and now and then tossed her hair behind her shoulders. So what?

Jessie Knowles brought coffee and went away. I felt at ease, but it was not simply a sense of relief. There was something new in the atmosphere of the cockpit.

We flew on through the bumpy clouds, more aware than usual of the eerie beauty of the night and the throbbing of the 727's powerful engines. Old-timers think there is no longer any romance in flying. If you're not in an old biplane with the wind singing in the baling wires and tearing at your goggles, you're not flying. Many famous fliers have written about the joy and the wonder of flight from days long gone.

Charles Lindbergh, Ann Morrow Lindbergh, Antoine de Saint-Exupery, Amelia Earhart—these people lived, breathed, and spoke the language of flying and knew the blessed immensity of the sky before it was mapped by jet trails. Nothing can match what they experienced.

Don't let anyone kid you though. Flying is still magic. Flying jets is exhilarating. It may not be as much of a thrill from the passenger seat, but up front, where the action is, the airplane is a marvelous man-made bird soaring through an element that we started to explore only in this century.

All-night flights are drudgery. And yet they're not. Sitting with bloodshot eyes and stiffening muscles, you see the sun set, the moon rise, and the sun rise again, and all the while the clouds are illuminated with colors that make your heart lift. It is worth the weariness. You forget that there is dirt and smoke down below, junkyards and poverty and despair. The sky is clean and radiant—a great living ocean of buoyant eddies and currents, sometimes violent with storms but never petty with malice, a world above a world—and you are in it in a tiny little capsule called the cockpit, looking out and down at miracles.

There is the aurora borealis, and there are the great bejeweled spectral shapes that are our stars and galaxies. Down below, ahead, is a tiny glint of light that becomes a brilliant sparkle, then a glittering carpet and then a welcoming city.

I was warm in the glow of that cockpit, feeling humble and exalted at the same time. It seemed as though there was nobody up there but the three of us, three people in a closed-in intimacy that has nothing to do with anything except our passion for flight.

Voices murmured. We began our descent. The magic glow below turned into Buffalo. Not the city of my dreams, but my temporary crew base. I had my airline job and I loved it!

Bonnie was hired by American Airlines in 1973 as a flight engineer on the Boeing 727 and retired as a captain on the B757/B767 in 1998. Enjoying a variety of things, Captain Tiburzi is living life to its max with her family and friends in New York.

Bonnie's new hire class at American.

Building the Coffin/Bombs
by Kathy McCullough

Building The Coffin

In any aviation accident there are always a number of mistakes made, not just one. Old, salty pilots call this phenomenon *building the coffin*. A coffin has six sides; count them:

> *Coffin side number one:* I'm flying across the country in my Cessna 140, from Colorado to Florida, after graduating college. I have over one hundred flight hours and I'm a little cocky. This common low-time pilot tendency to overestimate your abilities is a killer.

> *Coffin side number two:* I fuel up in Kansas, but I neglect to climb a ladder to visually check my gas tanks. I had old gauges with cork floats that

are inaccurate, so this is a major mistake on my part. The line boy hadn't "topped them off" like I had asked. So I take off with less fuel than I think I have.

Coffin side number three: The clouds are scattered. I pull back on the yoke, climb above them, and head east. As the clouds become more broken and solid in some areas, instead of turning around, I am busy looking at my map and finding radio frequencies, now that I can't see the ground. Doing a 180-degree turn is what I was taught to do in this situation. Foolishly I fly on. Shoulda, coulda, woulda....

Coffin side number four: The winds aloft are stronger than forecast. Or I should have paid more attention during my weather briefing. I can't get my navigational radios to tune. I can't figure out what's wrong. (I later learn that I'm drifting south so fast that I am out of range of all the stations I try. Thinking I'm further north, I'm picking the wrong ground stations and none of them work.)

Coffin side number five: I'm on top of a solid overcast, unsure of my position. Lost. My heart is racing. Now it *is* too late to turn back. I've got to get underneath the overcast and figure out where I am. My fuel gauges are bouncing off empty. *Are they really empty?* I don't have a clue because I never checked my tanks so that I could time my fuel usage.

I know the statistics. A pilot who hasn't been trained to fly using instruments has less than a minute before they develop vertigo and become disoriented inside the clouds without a horizon for reference. Still, I start a spiral turn through a small hole, going in and out of the clouds. I have no choice—there is no other way down. I quickly become confused and disoriented, so I level out. Catching my breath, I try again, praying, keeping my turn steeper so that I stay mostly clear of the clouds.

This time my turn works. I'm safely below the clouds. Eureka! I start looking for an airport or any familiar reference on my sectional map, but nothing matches. Unbeknownst to me, I'm over Arkansas instead of Missouri. I decide to look for an airport before my engine runs out of gas.

When I can't find an airport, I start looking for fields. I'm scared, but I can do this. I've practiced engine failures lots of times. I line up on a suitable pasture. Just before touchdown, I see the horses. I add power and climb, searching until I find another flat, grassy field. Most of the fields have power lines or obstacles. Finally, I find one I like.

I fly a modified pattern, with a steep descent, and land in the grass. I should have taken a college class in agriculture. The "grass" is tall alfalfa. It wraps around my wheels, almost causing me to ground loop. (A ground loop in a tail dragger is easy to do, and the saying is there are those that have and those that will. It is when the wing tip touches, whipping the plane to a stop.) I put both feet on the left brake and rudder pedal, trying desperately to keep the plane straight, but my right wing tip still sinks toward the ground. Miraculously, the wing levels as I come to a stop. Breathing fast, I open my door and step out. I stand there, getting my bearings—shaking.

A farmer and his hired man drove up in a pickup. They were congenial and didn't seem to mind that I'd ripped up their field. We checked the plane for damage, but there was none. They offered to call a local crop duster to bring some gas.

The farmer and his wife fed me grilled cheese sandwiches and Arkansas pickles. They introduced me to everyone in Clarksville, Arkansas. They showed me around their farm and their barn full of hundreds of turkeys. Now I'm worried anew. The one thing you don't want to do, I've been told, is fly low over a turkey farm because the turkeys panic and run into a corner and suffocate. The farmer told me not to worry—turkeys are so dumb they lose some to suffocation every day.

While I was eating lunch, the hired man mowed a runway, saying they were planning to cut the alfalfa next week anyway. The crop duster brought a few gallons of gas and offered to fly my plane down to his strip. I didn't know where his airport was, nor did I have much experience flying out of short fields, so I thanked him and said yes. As he took off, he almost hit the treetops, and I wondered if I'd made the right decision.

The farmer's wife gave me two bottles of Arkansas pickles as a souvenir of my visit and drove me to the duster's strip. Her husband was blind, so he couldn't drive. The duster topped off the plane, and this time I climbed up and checked the fuel level. I paid the crop-duster for the gas and taxied out for takeoff.

As I pushed the power in, the wheels stuck in the mud. The plane rotated in such a way that I was looking out the front windshield at the ground!

I quickly pulled the power off, and the tail settled back down. Slowly I pushed the power back in, accelerating gradually over the soft ground. I took off for Little Rock, Arkansas. *What a day!*

Coffin side number six (the lid): Thank goodness I didn't make one more mistake and close the coffin. I can't tell you how much safer I was as a pilot after this incident. The cockiness was replaced by a sense of elation. I'm alive!

Bombs

Taking off out of Seattle's Sea-Tac Airport as a 747 copilot for Northwest Airlines, I never guessed what the day would hold. The sky was clear and our freighter roared into it, waking up people below. We turned north and the controller gave us a clearance direct to Anchorage, Alaska. It was early morning and we were alone in the sky.

We leveled at 32,000 feet. I monitored the radios, and the captain unplugged and leaned his head back, tired after moving to a new house. The flight engineer was back making coffee and using the lavatory. It was a glorious day to be flying and I took everything in. Victoria, Canada, passed below us—we had vacationed there a few years back. I could see the ferries moving between Victoria and Vancouver. My kids had loved that ferry, especially the massage chairs.

And then.

"Our reports are that a light twin has just hit one of the twin towers in New York City," Air Traffic Control said. The controller was talking to another pilot on a different frequency.

What?

"No, no other information yet. It was either a twin or an airliner."

Surprised, I looked over at the captain. He was still unplugged. I told him what they were talking about and he just shrugged, uninterested. I kept listening.

Both towers had been hit. The flight engineer came back up front and I relayed the conversation to him. "What have you been smoking while I was gone?" he asked, laughing.

"At first they thought it was a light twin, then the report came in that it was an airliner, now they're saying two airliners."

Finally, the captain sat up straight in his chair. Now we were all listening to the radio. It was surreal. Air Traffic Control closed the continental United States airspace behind us as we flew north.

More reports came in as we flew on to Anchorage. A Delta Air Lines flight was arriving from Tokyo, landing in Portland, Oregon. Seattle Center informed them that the continental United States was closed and asked them where they wanted to land.

"Portland, Oregon, sir," came the reply. They had not heard.

"Ah, Delta, I repeat, Portland is closed, where would you like to go?"

The Delta pilot did not sound flustered, just tired. He had, after all, been up all night. He repeated that Portland, Oregon, was his destination.

"Delta, the whole continental United States is closed. Pick another place to land."

A long silence followed. Finally, the Delta pilot answered, "Vancouver." Then, worried that he would be misunderstood, he quickly added, "Canada. Vancouver, Canada, sir."

The controller rogered that, then had us switch frequencies. We were laughing uncomfortably but not at the Delta pilot. It was probably just to release tension regarding the whole situation. Nothing like this had happened before.

The sky was a ghost town. We were the only plane on the frequency, talking to the controller. He informed us that both towers had collapsed. We were incredulous. *Maybe they were damaged, but collapsed?*

Upon landing in Anchorage, we parked, collected our bags, and walked across the ramp. Everyone was somber. We went inside and were directed upstairs to watch the television coverage. Horrified we watched as the buildings fell, over and over, on replay. It had never occurred to us that airplanes could be used as *bombs.*

Everyone in the nation was in shock, but we, as pilots, had our paradigm shattered. I called home to inform my husband that I was fine. He told me to call the school to let the kids know. My eyes filled with tears as the kids in my daughter's class cheered when the secretary made the announcement that I was safe.

Shaken, we were driven to our hotel. Then, the flight engineer and I rented a car and drove south to Portage Glacier for the day. Unbeknownst to us, downtown Anchorage was being evacuated. A plane was arriving from Asia without radio communication and authorities feared the worst. My kids were watching, horrified, as the news reported this breaking development. It turned out to be nothing.

Flags flew at half-mast that night as I ate dinner. The waitress and I cried. Next, I went to Humpy's, a local restaurant and bar in downtown Anchorage. There must have been fifty airline employees filling the outside patio with raucous drinking and conversation. We were all stranded indefinitely. The captain begged off any activity and slept the better part of three days. The engineer was in his room resting because his back had gone out on him earlier that day while we were sightseeing. Mine did the same the next morning. Stress does funny things to a body.

Three days later we were deadheaded to Minneapolis, Minnesota; then deadheaded to Los Angeles to continue our trip. We were subdued and wary for the next week in Asia, but nothing else happened. The trip was uneventful, but we acted like sleepwalkers, numbly getting through each day. Cell phone covers were for sale in Singapore and Hong Kong proclaiming, "Bin Laden Hero." We weren't in Kansas anymore.

Things have changed since 9/11. Our security is tighter, but we were already on alert. Many years before there had been a plan to blow up eleven 747s out of Tokyo—The Bojinka Plot. It was thwarted, but Northwest Airlines had begun searching their airplanes routinely, matching bags to passengers, even way back then. The only thing that changed significantly for us after 9/11 was airport security. It was now a hassle, even for flight crews. Some pilots retired early rather than be subjected to constant scrutiny at security checkpoints. Most of us realized it was a necessary evil. We submitted, grumbling, acknowledging that anyone could get a flight crew uniform and fake identification. The rumor was still rampant that one of the terrorists had been a jumpseating "pilot." This would make all the cockpit door reinforcements a farce if a terrorist was already up front.

September eleventh was a wake-up call for all of us, but we also realized that pilots cannot control everything. People asked me if I was afraid to fly. I wasn't. I asked them if they were afraid of tall buildings. They looked at me without comprehending. More people were killed in the twin towers in New York City that Tuesday morning, September 11, 2001, than in any plane crash.

Kathy was hired by Northwest Orient Airlines in 1981 and flew the Boeing 727, DC10, and Boeing 747. Captain McCullough retired from Delta Air Lines and lives on her wheat ranch in Oregon with her husband. She loves traveling, writing, and photography. http://kathymccullough.photodeck.com/

Kathy's Cessna 140.

American Airlines Flight 49:
Paris to Dallas-Fort Worth
Beginning September 11, 2001
by Beverley Bass

There I was at 39,000 feet.
Every good aviation story starts with that preamble, but in my case it was chillingly so.

Our flight was the second leg of my copilot's Atlantic International Operating Experience (I.O.E.). I was a check airman for American Airlines. I was notified at the hotel that our departure from Paris would be delayed for two hours. *It happens,* I thought to myself. But that day I was especially looking forward to getting home to my family, husband, son, and daughter. When our Boeing 777 arrived, I was advised that four of the eight lavatories were inoperative. What a mess! An eleven-hour trip with only half of the potty facilities working. Of course they could not be repaired, but we also had only 155 passengers going with us. It was not optimum, but it was doable. Little did I realize how significant that this condition, along with the late departure, would become.

The day was beautiful and the flight was normal. Well, as normal as continuous teaching for the I.O.E. would allow. As we approached 40 degrees west longitude, the news of the impossible began to creep into the usually benign air-to-air conversation over the radio. We first heard that an aircraft had hit the World Trade Center. Seventeen minutes later we were told another, not yet identified, aircraft had slammed into the other tower.

What was happening?

Later we learned that New York's airspace was closed and we began contacting American Airlines' dispatch. We expected to be routed around the New York area, but we had plenty of fuel. *No big deal for our flight.* Then an unequaled aviation phenomenon began, something which, to my knowledge, had never happened before. We began seeing numerous aircraft, which turned out to be foreign carriers, leaving the North Atlantic tracts. Unbelievably, they were doing one-eighties and flying east.

Word then came that all United States airspace was closed. This prompted my call for the other first officer to come to the cockpit. We began planning to divert into one of the larger Canadian airports. We realized at that point that if we had not departed late, we would have been in New York airspace during the attack and the rest of this story would have been very different. Our dispatcher was also in the dark and could give us very little help. We did not know at that time that we would have no choice of airports. We even considered returning to Europe. Then we were told that we would be assigned a diversion airport as we passed 50 West. The Gander, Newfoundland, airport was nearest, and we were ordered to land there.

Now, what do I tell the passengers? I didn't go into much detail except to say, "There has been a crisis in the United States. All of the airspace is closed and we will be landing our airplane in Gander, Newfoundland." I waited until after landing to fill in the details; I wanted to avoid any reactions from the passengers that would make the flight attendants' preparations for landing and our security more difficult to manage.

We calculated that we would be overweight for landing. Now the decision to jettison or not to jettison what might be precious fuel, had to be made. I decided that an overweight inspection in Gander could be very difficult to arrange and gave the order to dump fuel down to the maximum landing weight. Sure enough, the first comment I received upon landing at Gander was, "Did you land overweight? We hope not!" *Good decision!* The fuel jettison prompted the longest instrument final approach that I have ever flown—a ninety-five-mile final approach for an ILS (instrument landing system) back course approach to runway 22. The weather was good, but the crosswinds were high and gusty.

The landing was perfect! (Just kidding.) We were the thirty-sixth out of thirty-eight wide-bodies to land, which is probably why hundreds of Gander residents were lined up around the airport perimeter on our final approach, watching a once in a lifetime (we hoped) occurrence. The jumbo jets that diverted into this small town in Newfoundland carried more than seven thousand passengers. We flooded their population of ten thousand like a tidal wave!

Taxi to parking was the first of many ground adventures. "Sardine" stacking began. We were directed to the general aviation ramp to park wing tip to wing tip among three other big aircraft: a DC10 and two L1011s. The ramp was full of FOD (foreign object debris) in the form of loose asphalt, wheel chocks, etc. I was very concerned for the safety of my engines which, in this case, could have been giant vacuum cleaners. Low power turns into parking positions was very difficult but necessary.

We shut down the engines and I immediately made an announcement telling the passengers everything we knew about what had occurred in New York and Washington, DC. By this time several passengers, including a lady who worked for a Dallas-Fort Worth news station, were able to reach their offices by cell phones. Those contacts actually gave us more information than we received from other sources. Cell phone communications became very difficult and it was several hours before I could contact my family to tell them that I was okay. We later heard that Delta Air Lines had contacted all of their crews' families, but I had no confirmation that American Airlines had done the same.

Gander set up a special radio frequency with which we communicated directly to Gander officials. I cannot say enough good about our Gander emergency control center contact, Geoff Tucker, and Pat Woodford at the Gander tower controller. They were courteous and unflappable in their consistent care for all their uninvited visitors. They rose to the occasion and performed above and beyond what we could have expected. As the day went on, we heard radio calls from other airplanes requesting supplies. Water, food, baby food, diapers, and all kinds of medicine were brought onboard the parked aircraft which by now had become very, very, tight-quartered motels. We even heard that several pets, including two chimps, needed care.

Evening brought a call for all captains, copilots, and pursers to attend a meeting with Gander officials at 2300 hours. A plan for the departure had been designed with instructions that European airlines would depart first. Of course, that plan put our departure at the end of this unlikely parade. So we would all have to move our aircraft in sequence. The departure plan briefing was complete. We had to give our requested fuel load for departure, and that was then conveyed to American Airlines Dispatch. Now we knew how we would depart but not when.

Taxicabs to the motel were as scarce as they are on Broadway in New York City during a heavy rain. But no problem, day and night, we were volunteered rides from everyone in Gander. Policemen and citizens extended travel help to all the crews. We rode back to the motel with complete strangers and got some much-needed rest.

September 13th. Day Three: Lessons in Waiting

Waiting became the order of the day. My room was next to the office in the Comfort Inn. I left the door unlocked so that we could use it as a makeshift command post. I encouraged my crew to drop by to discuss whatever was on their mind. From one of the conversations, I learned that a lady who had been on a British Air flight was desperately trying to get to Dallas-Fort Worth (DFW). Her grandmother was very ill, and this was the purpose of her trip. Then she was informed that her grandmother had died. This of course intensified her desire to go with us when we departed for Texas. She contacted me, and I told her that I would love to help her, but I couldn't take her because of the inflexible rules concerning exact passenger boarding. She indicated that the British Air captain had approved her transfer. I told her that he didn't have that authority, but I would try to help her. Extended conferences with American Airlines Dispatch produced what I thought to be permission to fly her to DFW. Unfortunately, I did not have written confirmation, which would jump up to bite me later.

Basic care and feeding of passengers included keeping them informed. The purser, our "speakers" (multi-lingual flight attendants), and I went to the Knights of Columbus Hall. When we arrived, I was taken aback by the mass of humanity on cots, sleeping bags, and blankets. The blankets came from our airplane, and the sight appeared to be a picture of the inside of a giant airplane. Our customers were in high spirits considering the conditions they were in. I noticed that they all appeared shaven and showered, compliments again of the great Gander residents who had opened their homes and private baths. I briefed the passengers, allowing time for the speakers to translate into French and Spanish. I think we gained their confidence as they realized we were doing our best to get them to their destinations. I was very careful not to guess at when we might depart. The passenger reactions were very good, and I felt a strong bond developing which has continued to this day. It struck me as funny that the menu for the day was beans, bread, and donut holes. What delicate cuisine!

God Bless Walmart! Several crew members and I became very weary of wearing our layover clothes. We were beginning to feel like snakes itching to shed our skin, so we went shopping for new duds. Rarely am I at a loss for words when complimenting our hosts, but the Walmart store's generosity was beyond description. They definitely took the top prize in unconditional giving. Absolutely amazing! By the way, I have never in my life enjoyed a new outfit more!

September 14th. Day Four: More Planning

Alert, alert! At 1400 hours, our expected six-to-eight-hour warning for departure was now only one and a half hours. We dressed in our finest and went to the airport. We were more than ready, but now we couldn't find all of our passengers. Remember the rule: We have to leave with the same people on the airplane. We couldn't, so we lost our slot time. *Dang it!* Later, the first officer let the passengers know that this tardiness could not be tolerated, and the frustration of the long wait surfaced somewhat. Some folks took exception to the "preaching," and I heard about it later, but everyone was in place and prompt from then on.

An 1800 meeting was called for the purpose of briefing a mass taxi operation to clear an alternate runway because severe complications had developed on two aircraft. Lufthansa's passengers had contracted food poisoning and their temporary quarters at a local firehouse had lost water service. *A health risk!* In addition, ATA's passengers were ninety-five Make-A-Wish terminally ill children. *And I thought we had it bad!* The bottom line was that those aircraft had to get out. Therefore all of us, the airplanes in their way, had to be moved. Remember airplanes were parked on every taxiway, ramp, and an inactive runway. So we would have to move our aircraft in sequence.

We also learned that the remnants of a hurricane were bearing down on the airport, which necessitated the clearing of a cross runway. Inbound aircraft needed the flexibility of landing on the runway with the optimum wind. The briefing was a very complete PowerPoint presentation engineered by the commander of a C-5. After being advised of the plan, we were told that movement of aircraft would begin early the next day. Pilots hate waiting, so several folks said, "Let's move them now!" *Great idea, right?* Wrong! The tower chief arrived just in time to tell us that the fog had moved in prior to the hurricane. Now the visibility was nearly zero. Oh well, tomorrow was another day.

We went back to our home-away-from-home for some pre-emptive sleep because we had been advised that the US airspace would open tomorrow. We stopped by the passengers' humble abode and told them all that we had learned. We told them that we could expect a six-to-eight-hour warning for departure. Be ready, we said, because security procedures were expected to take three-to six-hours. In addition, we asked them to observe a curfew at 2300 hours so that everyone could be ready for departure. As it turned out, we were very thankful that we had imposed that restriction.

September 15th. Day Five: Going Home (Maybe)

Alert, alert! At 0015 hours, our six-to-eight-hour warning for departure was now only forty-five minutes. The lady from British Air called to tell me that her captain had released her. I coordinated with American Airlines and emphasized that I wanted no trouble taking this new passenger when departure time came. Yes, everything was set! *Sure.* We were back at the airport and security checks began, and so did the storm. *Timing!* Timing has always been my strong point. The wind and rain appeared to be from an old movie with someone throwing buckets of water on us as we made our way to the airplane, but the forecast was good enough. There was hope of departure. What a day!

Finally through security! Man, that was easy—it only took six hours. We were beginning our security checks of the airplane, which we were told was our sole responsibility, when a male flight attendant approached me to say that the purser was very, very uncomfortable with two male passengers of Middle-Eastern descent. This was not the first time we had discussed these two men. During the inbound flight, one of the men had been refused more liquor by a flight attendant. He had become belligerent, stalked into the lavatory, only to return to his seat quite the gentleman. Quite a mood swing! I was told that one man had no carry-on bag. That was very unusual for a long trip. So, while in Gander, I had sent messages to American Airlines Security that I wanted a passenger manifest, by name, to investigate the men more thoroughly. The men's names were not on the first manifest. Strange. Many hours later, though, they had passed all American and local security checks. In fact, they were two of our most revered Platinum Club members. Hours had been spent with security making sure these guys were okay.

I had briefed the flight attendants on what I had done and thought that they were satisfied with the extra scrutiny of these men. But now we had a question, and I have a rule: Never go anywhere if every crew member is not completely comfortable. I never discount intuition! So, I called out the Mounties. I asked for a complete body and bag search. I told the police that I would watch as it was done. The two men were asked from the waiting lounge and, in private, the men were searched while I watched. Their one carry-on bag was emptied and searched. They were "spread-eagled" and I observed the most thorough body search ever. The men were quite cooperative, and I thanked them and continued to apologize to them until they rode out of sight after landing in Dallas-Fort Worth. It was necessary but that didn't make me feel any better for being so strict with these men who were perfect gentlemen. The flight attendants were briefed and comfortably accepted the security procedures that had been done.

By this time, we were past ready to go. The weather was nasty but somehow it seemed not to bother us too much. Finally we started up, taxied out, and were cleared onto the runway. We did not have our final load numbers, but we taxied onto the runway because the tower assured us that the next inbound airplane was forty-five minutes away. We waited, and waited, but we didn't receive a load closeout. Sure enough, the tower then asked us to clear the runway because the inbound aircraft was upon us. We cleared the runway and again queried American Airlines Dispatch about the delay. The reply was unbelievable at this point: The lady from the British Air flight was not on our manifest and, therefore, had to be deplaned! So much for an attempt at being kind to a fellow woman. Someone had dropped the ball, but it was I who had to taxi back to the ramp and leave the hysterical lady desperately trying to get to her grandmother's funeral. I later checked to see the outcome of her plight, but did not find out if she ever made it to Texas. I am very sorry about that.

Let's try it again. Taxi out was becoming routine. The weather wasn't better this time, but we had plenty of practice in ground operations. *Guess what?* We again waited forever for our load closeout. It seemed like a giant conspiracy. *What had we done to American Airlines Dispatch to deserve this?* All pilots think this way because we are so much better at going than we are at waiting. But I think, after what we had endured the last several days, our lack of patience was well deserved. At last, in the early, early morning, we took off.

First Officer B flew the leg because it was certainly his turn. Remember the bunks? We got some great safety rest going home. I crawled into the bunk not remembering the last time I had slept that well. When we crossed into the United States everything seemed better. I wanted to make one more appearance, walk through the cabin, and personally thank each passenger. To my surprise and delight they showered me with all kinds of gifts, greeting cards, T-shirts, and other souvenirs. The passengers and the flight attendants were very nice. It felt great in my descent announcement to say, "Welcome, not only to the great State of Texas, but to the United States of America!" We landed at DFW, and the first thing we noticed as we taxied to the ramp was the huge American flag on American Airlines' tower.

My emotions while in command of an airplane had never been so raw! When I saw that outpouring of patriotism upon our return, I will admit to almost losing it. We cleared customs to the flags, flowers, well wishes, hugs, and kisses of our airline friends and family.

As I drove away from the airport, my mind lingered on that great place: Gander, Newfoundland. The events that triggered our stay will remain in my mind for a long time, just like all American citizens. But the really indelible memories will be about the people of a small town who spared nothing, not even their hearts, to welcome us to their land.

In retrospect, my fondest memory is of two senior ladies who waited with us one dark and stormy night as we braved the rain and wind trying to return to our motel. Of course, they recognized us as Americans. None of us kept a dry eye as one of the ladies opened her bag. She pulled out a small accordion and began to play "God Bless America!" My response: "God Bless the people of Gander!" *I cried!*

I hope you understand that my purpose for writing this was to help me remember the historical events of that fateful week. Also, it was to thank the people of Gander. I have since sent two plaques with our flight number, names, and thanks to the airport personnel who were so kind and efficient with their help. My intent was also to record for scrutiny and critical analysis the job of an airline captain when we are called upon to do quite a bit more than just fly the airplane.

Editor's note: Some of Beverley's experience in Gander became part of the Broadway play, "Come From Away."

Beverley was hired by American Airlines as a flight engineer on the Boeing 727 in 1976. Captain Bass retired in 2008 on the B777. Beverley and her husband spend their free time traveling and enjoying their homes in Texas and Florida.

Jenn Colella (the actress who plays Beverley
in the play) with Beverley Bass.

Alaska Beckons
by Julie Clark

I n 1976 I was at an airport waiting for an incubator baby to be delivered to my air taxi airplane. Standing there, I was intrigued by an advertisement for the sale of surplus airplanes. This particular ad was in Trade-a-Plane: "For Sale: Auction by U.S. Government, two Forestry Department A-45s located in Anchorage, Alaska." I thought, *Wow. Who would read that and know it meant two Beech T-34 Mentors?* The average pilot doesn't know that particular military designation. The minimum bid was $17,000. All I could think was how much I'd enjoyed flying the T-34 at NAS Lemoore, and I remembered how sad I'd felt when I pulled the mixture back to cut the engine after my last flight. I sat in the quiet cockpit for a few minutes and thought, *I'll never have another chance to fly one of these airplanes again.*

Penny Becker, a pilot, a member of The Ninety-Nines, and a friend to whom I'd given a familiarization ride and taught to fly at Western Sierra, was the first person I called. Penny was my air race copilot when we got together to compete and bring home some trophies. I called Penny and told her how much I'd like to bid on the surplus airplanes in Alaska. When I lamented not having $17,000, she told me I didn't need to pay that amount to register the bid. Then she went one better: She found the necessary $1000 to place the bid and loaned me the money.

Without breathing a word of my plans to my husband Rick, I placed the bid and promptly forgot about it. *Wasn't it unwise to bring up the possibility of buying a T-34 before there was any certainty that, when the auction was over, I might be the highest bidder?* It was a challenge to judge the timing for broaching a sensitive subject with your spouse when trying to qualify for an airline job and just spending time together proved to be controversial. *Why not wait to talk about it when it looked as if the bid might actually win? Why start some sort of battle when the bid might come to nothing?* At the time, Rick had been hired by Hughes Airwest in what I perceived to be fabulous flying assignments, and this intensified my desire to be hired. My focus was on getting on with an airline, not fully appreciating that my being hired would speed up the graveyard spiral of an already strained marriage.

An Alaskan Bird

More than six months later, my secret sought the light of day when I received the response to my bid for the T-34, the "Warbird in Alaska." When I was notified about holding the winning bid, it was essential that I travel to Alaska to pay for and remove the aircraft. I'd almost forgotten about having made the bid, so when word came that I was to come to Alaska to fly it away, I was stunned. But, the shock was much greater to Rick, as he'd known nothing about the bidding process.

When I was notified of having won, once again, the first person I called was Penny Becker. She went from bank, to credit union, to bank with me—trying to find one single loan officer who was daring enough to risk a loan. When they asked, "Where is the airplane?" I said, "Alaska." When they asked, "What is its condition?" I said I hadn't seen it. When they asked, "What is its Blue Book value?" I had to tell them that surplus military equipment *has* no Blue Book rating. No wonder the loan officers refused! It was amazing that we finally found one trusting soul at Crocker Bank in Fresno who was willing to take the risk. They loaned me $14,000 and I breathed a huge sigh of relief.

The man next in line, who wanted both T-34s, was an aircraft restorer named Red Stevenson in Tulsa, Oklahoma. As I was the highest bidder, I got to choose between the two. I called the maintenance people to ask their advice and was told one plane "looked better," but the other was more "mechanically sound." Knowing that Red Stevenson wanted "my" airplane, too, the pressure was on for me to get to Alaska. Naturally, I had to tell Rick where I was going and what I was doing. The roof went off the scale! It was *ugly*. I doubted he even cared whether I made it back or not.

I was flying for Golden West on the 12th of July, 1977, and two days later, on the 14th of July, I arrived at Merrill Field in Anchorage via Western Airlines. Warned of the need for survival gear, a rifle, and emergency rations of food and water, Penny had again come to my rescue. She rented the equipment at a sporting goods store and had it shipped to Anchorage. I added some charts and navigational aids to help me in flying almost 3000 miles in an, as yet, unseen machine.

Early the next morning, I awoke to cold, depressing rain and fog and hired a taxi to Elmendorf Air Force Base to locate "my" T-34A. The military logos had been spray-painted over; however, the craft was an aluminum relative of the airplanes I'd been flying at Navy Lemoore. There were subtle differences between the A and B models, and all I had flown were T-34Bs. Although I knew the T-34B well, I didn't know this T-34A at all. *Two different models with just a few subtle differences.* The military told me that I didn't need the survival equipment. They assured me that I would be sitting on a complete survival kit located beneath my seat. So I then had to make arrangements to ship the equipment back to Penny.

Because the weather was below the minimums in which a pilot can legally fly according to Visual Flight Rules (VFR), my departure was held up for eight hours. When I finally departed, I flew through "Windy Pass" toward Whitehorse, Yukon. I got lost and finally determined, after aligning with the direction of a known runway, that my wet compass was at least forty-five degrees off from the rear compass. In Whitehorse, I was grounded in very bad weather, low ceilings, and poor visibility. I spent a restless, and uncomfortable night, sleeping on the floor of the women's bathroom in the terminal building. Upon discovering that the compass in the rear seat was accurate, I borrowed some tools and used the correct compass to replace the front-seat gauge.

The next morning, I departed for Watson Lake, Yukon. During my careful pre-flight, while looking at the nose of the airplane, which lacked a grill to cover the carburetor air filter intake, this gaping hole reminded me of the lopsided smile of a friend named Wally from my TWA days. He had helped me use an E6B computer at a time when few flight attendants were taking flight lessons. Believing that every airplane should have a name, my T-34 was thereby christened

"Wally." That afternoon, despite a rough engine, Wally and I limped on to McKenzie, British Columbia. While in flight down the Alcan Highway, known as the "Trench," a catastrophic event happened. The battery exploded due to an overheating situation and blew a hole through the side of the airplane. Battery acid leaked into the cockpit and, as the fumes spread, breathing became very difficult and I was forced to land. The fumes were bad enough, but the acid had also splattered on my clothes. It even ate portions of the zippers on my knee-high boots.

Mechanics later confirmed that the battery blew because of an overheating problem. They said, "We can get you started, but you're not going to have any electrical power." *How was the gear operated?* Electrically. *How were the flaps operated?* Electrically. *What did the radio depend upon?* Electricity!

The rest of the flight was tough. I had to operate to Prince George, British Columbia, without a radio (NORDO). Gear can be muscled down manually, but more challenging was that the gear couldn't be retracted. The extended gear created enormous drag all the way to California. Drag, in turn, forced the cylinder head temperatures to almost redline. The hotter the engine, the hotter the oil temps and the lower the oil pressure. All were indications that a pilot does *not* want to see. Flaps can be ignored, if precise airspeed control is maintained, so that was a relatively minor problem. But I had to navigate with nothing but a wet compass and a chart. Having no radio meant that I had to make telephone calls to tower operators ahead of my arrival in order to be expected in their airspace. I couldn't depend on the fact that there wouldn't be more surprises. I also had to count on landing at airports that had the capability of giving me 24-volt power starts, and that was a rarity. Most airports served general aviation aircraft that ran on 12-volt batteries.

Personally, I looked awful. My clothes—the same ones in which I'd left home—were splattered and stained by the battery acid, and my boots drooped toward my ankles like sloppy stockings. The airplane was a sight and my looks probably convinced people that we'd narrowly escaped a fate worse than death.

South of there, the flight was interrupted with a low oil pressure indication. I landed at Omak and had to add five quarts of oil before pressing on to Kingsley Field, Klamath Falls, Oregon—a joint-use military and civilian base. At Kingsley I landed first, and then I had to explain to tower operators about my radio silence. Despite oil problems, I pressed on to Red Bluff, California, and, on the 16th of July, reached Oroville, California. I had to clear customs on a very small dirt strip and then flew on to Fremont and San Carlos. I landed at Fremont to call on a landline to obtain permission to land in San Carlos.

In my logbook, I wrote, "Home, Praise the Lord."

Airborne the Next Day

I flew at Golden West the following two days with Captain Ron Reed. On the 17th of July, 1977, I flew two hops, and on the 18th of July, four hops, for a total of 5.3 hours of flying time. My enthusiasm was boundless and, temporarily, confrontations at home were held at bay. When the battery acid fumes had filled the cockpit, I had first thought, "I'm dead!" Then, I sort of shrugged and figured, "Oh well, Rick's going to kill me anyway. He's going to have my ass on a platter." I dreaded showing the airplane to him. It wasn't terrific mechanically, but it looked much worse than it was. I stopped in Fresno to see him, but I dreaded hearing his comments.

Among other things, he said, "I can't believe you bought *that*. I can't believe you went all the way to Alaska and brought *this* back." I was headed for Los Angeles; he was going back to Las Vegas. I got Wally home, but I didn't know where I was going to park him. I didn't have a tie-down site, and I had to get back to Golden West. I also had a furious husband. I knew he'd be right if he said, "You brought this all on yourself."

It was another low point of my life.

Wally and I had safely flown for 21 hours. But home wasn't ever going to be the same again. Did Rick, born on the 1st of November under the sign of Scorpio, fulfill the zodiac descriptions? "Scorpios are the most intense, profound, powerful characters in the zodiac. Even when they appear self-controlled and calm, there is a seething intensity of emotional energy under the placid exterior. They are like the volcano, not far under the surface of a calm sea." Rick was not perfect. Few people are, but Wally and I were pushing my Scorpio to his limits.

Today: Forty years later

Today, the name "Julie Clark" is a household name in the air show industry. I've just finished flying my 37th consecutive year on the circuit, in the same trusty T-34. After nearly thirty years as an airline pilot, I've now been retired for over ten years and still relish every flight in my beloved T-34—an airplane that I spent four and a half years restoring. Wally and I have now flown nearly 11,000 hours together. He is definitely my favorite "dance partner"!

Julie was hired by Golden West Airlines in 1976 and retired in 2003 from Northwest Airlines as an Airbus 320 captain. Julie has *not* retired from aerobatics and is still thrilling spectators at air shows in her Beechcraft T-34 Mentor.

Flying the Boeing 747
by Lynn Rippelmeyer

B-747 Training

"**H**ow would you like to be the first woman in the world to fly the 747?"

I looked across the desk at Captain Carl Hirshberg, whom I had just met. Was this a trick question, testing my knowledge, seeing if I knew my limitations? Maybe it was his idea of a joke to break the ice.

I had accompanied Jack, my fiancé, to his pilot interview at a JFK cargo building. When it got dark and cold waiting in the car, I found my way to the small office labeled Seaboard World. A friendly receptionist named Alice invited me to wait with her, saying Jack was still talking to her boss, Captain Carl Hirshberg, whom she referred to as "the silver eagle." She was full of questions and soon learned that I was also a pilot, lived nearby on Long Island, and was recently furloughed from TWA where I had worked as a B-727 flight engineer. As I answered her questions, she worked at her desk, writing on a pad of paper. She encouraged me to interview, too. I countered that the furlough would only last three months, I was recently engaged, and I wanted to spend some time with my fiancé. Besides, I was dressed in jeans and a sweatshirt, as we were on our way to a casual dinner. Still, she insisted I just pop in to say "hi" to her boss before I left.

Alice preceded me into the chief pilot's office and laid her notepad on his desk. Carl was a strikingly handsome man in his fifties, with a dark tan, blue eyes, and silver hair. It was the silver hair that I assumed gave him his nickname. He had the bearing of a man used to being in charge, getting what he wanted. He motioned for me to sit in a chair facing him across a desk where model airplanes portrayed the history of Seaboard World Airlines. The latest ones were a DC-8 and a B-747. I noticed the 747 had no passenger windows. I considered the 747 the most beautiful plane made. Most pilots agreed, making her the favorite and most senior choice at the airlines lucky enough to include her in their fleet. Eight years earlier, in 1972, I had begun my airline career as a flight attendant on TWA's newly arrived jumbo jet.

I looked from the planes to the man as he finished reading what I assumed were Alice's notes. He looked up, still waiting for an answer to the question I was still trying to decipher.

"Well, what do you say? Ready to break new ground?" he urged. His smile seemed genuine. Maybe this was his attempt at a humorous introduction to make me more comfortable.

I spoke what I knew to be true. "Women can't fly the heavies."

His smile faded. "Who told you that?"

"The guys at TWA," I responded quickly and went on to explain. "It takes too much strength if two engines were to go out on one side."

I had heard this argument often, stated as fact, during the year I worked in the B-727 cockpit. As the second female pilot to be hired at TWA, I got to hear a lot of reasons why women shouldn't be there. The male pilots proclaimed women to be unfit and incapable physically, mentally, psychologically, and emotionally—especially during "that time of the month." I knew all of it to be untrue except the physical strength part. No woman had ever flown the larger aircraft, referred in a group as "heavies." What if it were true? It was good to know and admit one's limitations, I thought.

"That's hogwash!" Captain Hirshberg exclaimed, his bright smile returning. "It's all hydraulics. I'll show you."

He asked a few more questions about my personal and professional background and as suddenly as it had begun, the "interview" was over. He ushered me, dazed and confused, into the hall saying, "Thanks for stopping in. We'll be in touch."

Seaboard World was a cargo airline using DC-8s based in London and B-747s based at JFK in New York to transport cargo around the world. Unlike other airline crews, Seaboard's flight engineers, the people in the cockpit helping the two pilots, preferred to remain in their own union and third-seat position instead of upgrading to a pilot seat. Therefore, anyone hired as a pilot went directly to the first officer, or co-pilot, seat. Because the pilots based in London didn't have to pay US income tax, the DC-8 was the favorite, more senior plane. At Seaboard, unlike anywhere else, the most junior pilot position was that of a B-747 first officer. A female hired by Seaboard would become the first woman to fly "The Whale."

Two weeks after our interviews, Alice called while I was vacuuming the pea green shag carpet in our Miami apartment. She was really excited to invite me to a training class the following month. Jack, however, having only a two-year degree and no Stanine test results was not hired. I refused the offer, repeating my previous reasons. She was disappointed and said she would wait to give the captain my answer. She suggested I think it over and call back.

I returned to vacuuming, but I couldn't stop thinking, "I could be flying a 747," as I went through my daily house chores. The no-win, inner dialogue plagued me day and night. How could I pass this up? If Jack loved me, he would support my career, as I would his, right? If it was meant to be, we would work it out—hopefully. If not, it was good to know that now. If I didn't take it, would I resent him forever? If I did, would he resent me? Would he and others respect me as a career pilot if I turned it down? Should I risk sacrificing my relationship or my career? Men didn't have to make these choices.

The conversation with Jack was much briefer than the ones I'd had with myself, because he had evidently already come to his own conclusion. Of course, he agreed, I had to take the job. It was the opportunity of a life time. But I also had to return his grandmother's ring and take a taxi to the airport. It was one of the most gut-wrenching decisions I have ever had to make. It left me sick for a month. Fortunately, the ground school was an effective distraction and eventually life went on.

The mechanics who taught our ground school explained the two, three, and sometimes four backups to every system that allowed the 747 to continue flying safely even on just one engine. The innovative eight-wheel, trunked, gimbaled landing gear made landings the smoothest passengers had ever experienced. A state-of-the-art (at the time) triple-channel INS system allowed excellent navigation ability and landings to the lowest allowable minimums. The auto roll-out, auto-reverse, and braking features seemed futuristic. She was art, interactive art, and I got to know her inside and out. One friend who saw me studying the four-colored schematic of the hydraulic system had it reproduced as modern art and hung it over her couch. However, I got to do more than just admire its beauty—I got to fly her!

Seaboard didn't have its own training center, so they rented simulator time from United and American but used their own instructors. The 747 was the first jet I had flown, so there was a steep learning curve. However, I thought it was the perfect place to start. As the latest and most modern aircraft, her designers were able to build on all the technology and knowledge that had gone into previous models, creating a much improved and simplified product. After working on the B-727, I marveled at all that Boeing had accomplished in this, the queen of their fleet.

There was a slight problem during my simulator training when my instructor decided that his nineteen-year-old son, whom he thought should have been hired instead of me, deserved half of my simulator time and brought him along to our sessions. He reasoned that when I failed, my replacement would be ready to step in. He also thought it would be fun to do aerobatics, which caused the sim to jump off its supporting jacks, and then he blamed it on the "girl trainee." Captain H came to the rescue and finished my training in record time.

From the simulator, we went to Wichita, where the airplanes' C-checks were done. During these test flights, the airplane's warning systems were activated to ensure all functioned correctly. I got to fly those test flights, taking a 747 to the limits in all configurations. We did steep turns, dives and climbs, checking every red-line warning. It was amazing to see something that huge be so responsive and graceful, even in the worst of conditions. After pulling back on the yoke to keep the nose up and demonstrate a stall with horn, clacker, and stick shaker sounding, I was instructed to just let go and watched as her nose came down to allow the wind over her wings once more, catching herself as if on a cloud, gliding into recovery—and we did it again and again, losing minimal altitude each time. I left with the utmost confidence in this beautiful machine.

The final checkride was done in the real plane, empty except for the FAA inspector, Captain H, and me. Taking off at midnight from JFK, we flew to Atlantic City, where we had the whole place to ourselves. Under a starlit sky, we warmed up with instrument approaches and crosswind landings.

Because the outboard engine housing is so close to the ground during crosswind landings, the usual upwind wing low maneuver on touchdown isn't advisable. Again, the unique gear system solved the problem and helped the pilot with a smooth, successful outcome. Keeping the plane "crabbed" until seconds before touchdown was a new habit I learned that initially made me nervous. Noticing my apprehension during training, Captain H had me practice them over and over repeating, "You LIKE crosswind landings," until I had to admit, it was true.

I wasn't sure when the warm-up stopped and the checkride began during our two hours in the air. I just continued complying with the requests to perform maneuvers and instrument approaches while wearing a hood to prevent me from seeing outside, thereby relying solely on the array of instruments inside. Captain H had done a great job preparing me for this day and was performing the duties of my co-pilot. All was going well and as rehearsed. We were on what should be the final ILS three-engine approach when Captain H unexpectedly called out, "Truck on the runway. Go around."

It surprised me so much that I looked up and out the windshield—a definite no-no while being evaluated. The star-lit night was perfectly clear, as was the runway. I was so close to landing and being done. "No there's not," I argued.

"Wrong response. Yes, there is. Go around." I thought I had done a near perfect job on this last exercise, demonstrating an engine fire and shut down, fuel dump, holding, and all that went with it. I was on the home stretch. But now, for some reason, someone wanted to see it again. I pushed the throttles to near max power, compensated the uneven thrust with the rudder and executed the go-around.

"Tell tower we are on the missed and want a straight-out departure." I began the process we had already done once when I felt a power change and needed even more rudder to continue going straight. Then, I saw warning indicators light up and dials move.

"Engine failure," Captain H called out as he retarded the throttle, simulating a failure of the second engine on the same side. I now had the situation I had been told a female couldn't handle. Damn. Why would he do this to me? Was it the FAA's idea? Did they want me to fail? Well, that wasn't going to happen.

The anger and adrenaline put all the strength in my leg to help take the rudder pedal to the floor as I kept the huge plane climbing on the same heading. I had to lock out my knee and brace myself until we got to pattern altitude where I could ease off a bit as the power came back and we began yet another approach in an abnormal configuration. By the time we were on final approach and I was calling for "gear down," my voice was shaking from irritation, frustration, and exhaustion. I thought he was here to help me, and the FAA guy had seemed nice enough. I knew I didn't have to perform that maneuver to receive my certificate. This scenario had never happened to the real plane, and we had never practiced it. Why would either of these men want to embarrass me now? I put it out of my mind and concentrated on setting the power correctly to configure the plane for landing, following the instruments that led me down the glideslope to the runway.

"Small movements and changes," I told myself as I struggled to stay on course. It was one of the many things Captain H had taught me. It minimized rudder input changes and prevented a vicious cycle of over-corrections, putting the pilot behind the plane and feeling like they were just along for the ride. The approach and landing went well—not perfect but well within parameters, and we made it to back to the ramp safe. Sometimes, like now, that's the definition of a good flight—no blood: no bent metal.

The FAA guy deemed it a good flight, too, and handed me the precious certificate that declared me a 747 pilot. He congratulated me on a good job and the fun evening. Pilots have a strange definition of "fun." I waited until he left the cockpit before confronting my mentor turned-traitor.

"Why on earth would you do that to me?" I asked in a measured, angry tone. Refusing to face my betrayer, I stared straight ahead at the empty ramp and continued my rant.

"Two engines out? Same side?" I put my hands under my thighs to stop them from shaking. I wasn't sure I was going to be able to stand up. My leg felt as dead as those engines.

"I thought you were going to help me," I said more quietly.

Still feeling hurt by his lack of loyalty and consideration, I turned to see him smiling at me. With fatherly affection, he calmly stated, "I'm not having you up there thinking you can't do something that you can do. You're welcome. And—congratulations!"

I thought of our first conversation and all he had done during these months of training.

All I could say was, "thank you," and I meant it with all my heart.

I flew the 747 for Seaboard World from 1980 to 1981 when it merged with Flying Tigers and I was furloughed. The next year, I found employment at a new airline, People Express, where I upgraded to B-737 captain. When PEX acquired 747s in 1984, I transitioned to the left seat of my favorite plane and became the first woman to captain the jumbo jet across the Atlantic.

Many of my subsequent flights were memorable for a variety of reasons. The main components of the job—people, weather, machinery—are never the same or predictable from one day, one flight, to the next.

However, one flight, one night stands out when I heard Captain Hirshberg's words again.

I remember it as if it were happening now.

A Three-Engine Night

The ringing sound pulls me from a deep sleep and is accompanied by the adrenaline rush familiar to international pilots flying "on the dark side of the clock." I hit the alarm button and look around for clues. My room or a hotel? AM or PM? What day, country, reason for the ringing that won't stop? Oh, the phone.

"Hello?"

"Captain Rippelmeyer?" Of course, it was scheduling. Who else would call in the middle of the night? I sit up and try to shake off the deep sleep. I had stayed up late so that I would sleep later in the morning to prepare for a London trip the next night. The clock says 1:30. What does that mean? Had I slept all day and missed my check-in? Another rush of adrenaline hits.

"Yes. That's me. Is it tomorrow already?"

"No. Well, actually, yes. It is Saturday now. We need you to fly to London. How quickly can you get here?" I was waking up but still confused.

"Now? It's Saturday already? Did I miss check-in?"

"Oh. Sorry." The scheduler finally realizes my confused state and slows down.

"Here's the scene. We need you to fly the flight that was scheduled for tonight. Friday. It took off but had to do an air return, and the cockpit crew is out of time to be legal, so we have to re-crew. The flight attendants have agreed to stay and go out again, and all of the passengers are still here. Maintenance says they will have the plane ready to go in two hours. Think you can make it?"

It was starting to sink in. I had been asleep for an hour and half and was now going to fly to London sooner instead of sleeping to prepare to do it much later in the day. The FAA has regulations that made the original crew illegal to continue, but no such rules apply to the flight attendants. I hoped they were getting some rest during this delay. It was going to make for a very long night.

"What happened?" I hold the phone to my ear as I got out of bed and began putting on the uniform hanging ready on the door knob.

"The filter bypass light on the #3 engine came on. They were concerned it was engine oil contamination and were only two hours out, so they opted to do an engine shutdown and return.

Turns out it was just a gauge problem and it had been replaced, so we should be good to go as soon as we can get a crew here to fly."

"OK. I'm on my way." No traffic. Terminal parking. I quickly calculate. "Should take about forty-five minutes." I hang up without saying goodbye. He'll understand. No time for niceties.

I was glad I had showered, washed my hair, and brushed my teeth before retiring for the night. I rationalized skipping makeup by assuming everyone will be too bleary eyed to notice. I grabbed my flight bag, overnight suitcase, and wheelies that wait packed and ready by the door, and hoped the car had enough gas to make it to the airport.

I met the rest of my crew in the dispatch room where the flight's paperwork was waiting for my approval and signature. The flight engineer, Jim, is clearly not pleased with being here and makes it known. Mutiny before even having launched is not good. Fortunately, the first officer, Pete, and I have flown as a crew before and we work well together.

One of the many things I like about this career is that I get to fly with different people on every trip, which means I get to hear their stories and their views. I've always found people fascinating, and pilots are a unique breed. I wonder briefly if Jim's attitude is due to having his sleep disrupted or to having me as his captain. Since he's not making eye contact and is only answering with one-word answers, I assume the latter. At this point, I've been an airline pilot for seven years and a captain for three, but in 1984, the term "female pilot" is still an oxymoron to some. To fly with a female pilot was a rare occurrence, as we were less than 1% of the pilot population. And female captains were less than 1% of that number, and on the 747, there were only two of us in the world. Jim was probably thinking, "Why me?"

During the late 1970s, as the major airlines began to comply with EOC anti-discrimination laws, female pilots were finally introduced to the pilot ranks. Acceptance was hard won, granted only after proving oneself. I was used to the initial negative reaction after being one of the first females at two previous airlines.

We women heard a whole litany of accusations and reasons we should not be allowed a flight crew position: We were taking jobs away from men and food from the mouths of babes; we were a distraction, incompetent, causing men to do their job plus ours, and therefore dangerous; a disruption to the natural order of things; a waste of the airline's time and money to train since we would quit or wash out and could never upgrade to captain. Personally, I thought the main problem was the fear of having their macho mystique destroyed. If a 5'4" 120-pound female could fly, how hard could it be?

Now, after four years at People Express (PE), confrontations here were rare. Most PE employees were in their twenties and thirties, more open to the changing attitudes of the times, including the women's liberation movement. Many pilots had wives in the corporate world and even seemed to enjoy the gender mix in the workplace. It was a good environment to first step into the role of captain; however, it was still a world unknown. There was no one to call for advice, no mentors to follow into these uncharted waters. I had wonderful training, and I had support from my instructors and peers. However, as a female, I found I had a much finer line to walk in fulfilling the role of captain than my male counterparts. A captain has to be commanding. There could be no question of who was in charge when making decisions. Especially in an emergency, the roles had to be clear from the start. If I was too soft, my competence was questioned and challenged. But if I was too hard, I was a bitch. Sometimes, with some people, that fine line was impossible to find or walk.

Some guys would say they were used to the idea of female pilots as long as they knew their job and followed instructions—from them. However, the idea of a female giving them orders, being the captain, didn't sit well. I had learned to handle it, usually successfully, and I hoped that would be the case with Jim tonight.

I am glad Pete is here. Retired military, he is older and more experienced than I, but since he was hired later, he is junior to me and a first officer. He understands the need for our roles to be specific and clear. He has always been excellent in the right seat, supporting me as captain.

Pete and I discuss our upcoming flight, trying to include Jim in the paperwork's information: fuel load, weight and balance, alternate destination, weather, flight plan, Atlantic crossing airway, the ATC clearance. Jim's attitude improves a bit, but he is still not a happy camper. A call to the maintenance chief assures me that the gauge problem has been resolved and checked with an engine run-up. There should be no more problems. The plane is refueled and the passengers boarded. I check in with the flight attendants to thank them for hanging in there for another go at this and to give them the pertinent information: time *en route* and weather. Many flight attendants are my good friends in this small airline. As a former TWA flight attendant, I know their job isn't easy. I like to show them the respect and understanding they deserve as part of the crew.

Everything is looking good in the cockpit, except for the fact that it is 4 o'clock in the morning. We are the only plane talking to ground, tower, departure, and ATC control as we take off and level off at 33,000 feet. It is a beautiful clear night, decorated with city lights below and stars above. We leave the eastern seaboard behind, heading toward Halifax, our next waypoint.

Two hours after take-off, the sky is turning shades of purple and pink. The tip of a red gold orb rises from the waters, defining the horizon, as we continue east over the Atlantic.

The twinkling stars outside are fading as a light inside starts blinking. It is labeled "Eng Oil Press" for the #3 engine.

"Did you see that?" Pete says, pointing at the offending bulb.

I respond with something articulate and commanding like, "Oh shit."

I look at the engineer's panel hoping to see evidence that it is only the erroneous indicator returning to haunt us. However, I also see the #3 engine oil gauge needle bobbing from green to yellow with the same rhythm that the light up front is blinking. They are both wired to the same sensor, so maybe it's a bad sensor, I think, ever the optimist. However, the #3 oil quantity gauge that should read between 6 and 7 gallons is pegged out below 1. Two bad sensors? Not likely. I ask Jim to pull the indicator CBs to see if they are powered and working. Yep. All indications show that we dumped seven gallons of oil in two hours. Checklist time.

"Number three coming to idle."

I call out my actions so they can be confirmed by the crew. Throttle at idle—no change.

In fact, the needle is heading through the yellow arc to the red line.

"Watch me on three." I move my hand from the throttle to the fuel cut-off lever.

"You've got it," Pete responds. All indications show a good shutdown.

We are now running on three engines. The 747 is a beautiful machine and my favorite plane, an opinion shared by most who have been lucky enough to fly her. The three working engines can supply everything necessary for us to continue flying so that the plane can safely return to Newark—again.

I turn to look at Jim, sitting at the flight engineer panel. "Call Newark operations and maintenance. Tell them we are returning, that we have indications of no oil in #3 engine and an ETA of two hours from now." Now he really doesn't want to be here, and it shows in his, "Yes, ma'am." I wonder if he's adding "a female in control of it all" to his list of things that could go wrong and did. But as long as he does his job, he can think whatever he wants.

To Pete I say, "Tell ATC we're returning to Newark and need a lower altitude. Ask for 2-4-0. Check the chart for our three-engine altitude performance at this weight."

He already has the chart in his hand. We are heavy with fuel that would have burned off by the time we got to London but now puts us over landing weight for Newark and too heavy to stay this high with only three engines.

I retrim the rudder as we crab through the air with two engines pushing us on one side and only one on the other. Moving the rudder by applying pressure to the pedal keeps us going straight and the trim holds it there so I don't have to. The trim needs to be adjusted as the engine's settings change, which is almost constant as we turn and descend.

Everything is going smoothly. People wouldn't even know if I didn't tell them. The flight attendants, feeling the one-eighty turn and descent, call up to find out what is going on. I promise to be the one to break the bad news to the passengers. I can't even imagine what these people must be thinking after going through this twice in one night. In my best captain's voice, trying to sound calm and in control, I attempt an explanation they can understand.

"Folks. This is Captain Rippelmeyer. I'm sorry to be the one to give you more bad news tonight, but we are heading back to Newark. That same engine that was a problem before is even worse now. It has no oil. And, like your car engine, it can't run without oil, so we have shut it down. The 747 is a wonderful plane and very able to continue flying on three engines, but not all the way to London. So we are already heading back and should have you on the ground at Newark in less than two hours."

I wish that I'd had more of an explanation myself. Why did a gauge problem turn into a much worse engine problem? We would find out later that an oil return line got crimped when maintenance closed the cowling on the engine after changing the gauge. The crimp caused an oil leak. At the moment, however, the reason doesn't really matter.

David, the lead flight attendant comes up to give and get more detailed information. He offers me coffee and a Danish. No thanks. I just had a cup of adrenaline, am wired already, and can't risk needing the bathroom in the next few hours, and I'm more than a little busy trying to go over all the considerations for landing. We're too heavy.

"We need to dump fuel down to landing weight," I say. Being careful to keep the fuel load balanced, Jim sets up the panel to dump 10,000 pounds or 1666 gallons out of the wing tanks into a cross-feed line and out dump valves on the tip of each wing. It's supposed to atomize at 6000 feet, which should give it plenty of room from 24,000, but I want it done before we are over Boston, our first spot of land. He is doing a good job with the fuel as I double-check the progress and say, "Looks good." But there's more to do. "When you're done with the fuel, we need to review affected systems and procedures for a three-engine landing."

Jim nods. "Hydraulics are going to be an issue," he reminds me. "With only three pumps instead of four, the flaps and gear will take longer to come down." He seems to be more with the program now and part of the team, which is good because this is going to take all of us working together. The last thing I need is for part of my brain to be worried about him doing his job while I'm trying to do mine. We all agree we will want the full approach, not the short-cut visual they usually offer, and the longest runway, 4 Right.

When we check in with the next ATC controller who is watching our plane as a blip on his screen, Pete relays our situation, ending with, "No, no need for emergency equipment. Just need the longest runway." ATC tells us to start our descent.

Both of the guys are good at their jobs and are working well together and with me, pooling information, ideas, suggestions, and getting all the pieces together. The checklists help, but every situation is different and takes some adjustments. We're doing okay, I think, as I remember the point of CRM training: part of the captain's role is to create an environment conducive to input and help. It's clear why. This is definitely a team effort. In fact, it's feeling like a checkride in a simulator where they keep compounding the problem once you have the first one under control. I wonder what's next. I double-check all the system and engine indications. Other than some readings being a bit higher than usual and some at zero due to the one engine out, all looks good. We're on the home stretch as ATC hands us over to approach control.

"Approach, People one-ten heavy with you. We have the number three engine shutdown and want 4 Right for landing and the full approach." "Heavy" is a term added to the call sign of a wide-bodied aircraft like the 747 because of the extra wake turbulence it creates.

"Uh, People one-ten heavy, 4 Right is closed for resurfacing. Winds are three-two-zero at 19 knots gusting to 26. Runway 29 is in use."

If we were in a simulator, I'd be giving the instructor a dirty look for this unnecessary complication of a maximum crosswind. Unfortunately, there's no dial behind me to adjust the wind. It's going to be "sporty," requiring some fast rudder work due to the engines' uneven thrust and the crosswind, both of which will vary during the approach.

We ask for 4 Left, a bit shorter than 4 Right, but longer than 29. It has more crosswind, but also more concrete for stopping. The wind will be 90 degrees off the nose, directly on our left side. We'll have to be in a crab, pointing to the side of the runway until just seconds before touchdown, when rudder pressure will bring the nose around to point down the centerline and the left wing will go down just a bit to offset the cross-control and to keep the wing from lifting, but not too much because that outer engine nacelle is so close to the concrete runway.

A classmate of mine had recently scraped an engine nacelle on landing, causing sparks to fly. The tower called for emergency equipment, and they temporarily closed the airport. Rumor immediately spread that it was "one of the girls" at the controls. It bothered me more than it should have and I didn't want them to be correct.

I put anything negative and doubts out of my mind. I remember my training and I can hear Captain Hirschberg now: "Take your time and think. You have all the information, training, and ability. You are good at this. What's one less engine? You still have three. **You like crosswind landings**." I have to smile at the memory and imagine him sitting to my right.

It's 8:00 a.m. now. The world below is awake. It seems like ages since I've slept.

Approach tells us to descend to 6000 feet. We ask for 4000 in order to stay out of the cloud layer and the bumps. Checklists are done, special procedures and situation reviewed, everyone has been notified. Passengers are buckled in and ready for their second unscheduled arrival in Newark. We have kept them informed, and the flight attendants are doing whatever they can to make the experience as painless as possible. Everyone seems to be taking it as well as can be expected.

Each time we descend and level off, the power changes cause the rudder to be adjusted—which is the only real inconvenience of one less engine. The needle positions seem strange, different than usual with three engines having to do the work of four. Funny, the little things that you get used to seeing, feeling, and hearing that give you a sense of normalcy and comfort. Approach offers the "visual," allowing us the option to see the airport, go directly to it, and create our own speed and altitude pattern to successfully land, which I usually love. It saves time and fuel and is more fun to do without directions from Tower. This time, however, I'll take all the help I can get, and I ask for the full Instrument Landing System (ILS) which will give us guidance and help us stay established on the correct slope and path to the runway. We are handed off to Tower who gives us an intercept heading to join the localizer outside the marker where we pick up the glide slope. The flaps are taking longer to extend than usual at each setting due to the reduced hydraulic pressure. I try to keep the throttle and trim adjustments minimal. The gear comes down fine and all is looking good. The wind is so strong off my left that I'm seeing the runway ahead through the first officer's window, flying sideways to the threshold.

Jim makes the callouts as we descend toward the runway: "Landing Checklist complete. Flaps are at 30. 500 feet. Cleared to land. Ref +10. Sink 700 feet per minute. 400 feet. Ref+10 Sink 700. 300 feet. Ref +15. It's gusty down here. Sink 600 on speed. 200, 100, 50."

I pull gently back on the yoke to begin the flare as I hear, "Thirty feet." I gradually pull the throttles back to idle with my right hand, while my left hand on the yoke is commanding the aileron down to help in the fight against the wind trying to raise the left wing. We should be just a few feet above the runway now. I put the left wing down just a smidgen more as

I apply rudder pressure and tell the flight engineer to take out the rudder trim. A gust pushes us to the right side of the runway. This plane needs the whole width. I decrease the rudder input just a bit to get back to center and lower the nose so we can get on the ground quickly as the threshold goes beneath us. It works. A nice smooth touchdown for the sixteen tires that make up the main landing gear, but we aren't done yet. With the 747, there are actually two touchdowns—one for the main gear and a second for the two nose wheels, which also have to be flown onto the runway. As I'm using the rudder to bring the nose around to center, a gust lifts the left wing and the left gear leaves the runway. The flight engineer calls out as I add more aileron, and Pete reaches for the yoke to help if needed. I realize I haven't heard the familiar sound of speed brakes extending automatically and see the handle still stowed. Maybe they didn't deploy because of the hydraulic problem or because the left gear became unweighted. The reason isn't really important right now. I call out, "Speed brake!" as Jim is already reaching for it to deploy them manually.

With full left aileron deflection, I keep the left wing down and, with the rudder pedal, bring the nose around to touch down on the centerline. I see Pete backing me up on the yoke. My right hand goes from the throttles to the reversers and I yank back. Number three won't budge.

Of course, it's shut down. Which means I also can't have number two, the inboard engine on the other side, or I'll have asymmetrical reversing and risk leaving the center of the runway. "70%," Jim says, as I stand up the two outer levers to deploy the reversers on engines one and four.

That's all I can have. Slowing down is taking longer with only half the usual power.

The heavy weight plus the wind demanded a high approach speed which makes for a longer stopping distance. The end of the runway is coming up too quickly. We touched down doing 160 knots. Now, Jim calls out, "100 knots, 90, 80." It is taking way too long between each call out, not the comfortable, familiar rhythm I'm used to hearing.

I take over the automatic braking manually by pressing on the brake pedals as smoothly and firmly as possible. I see Pete sit forward, also sensing the need to slow more quickly. We take the last high-speed turnoff onto the taxiway at fifty knots and continue to slow to taxi speed.

We made it! But we are far from done.

"After-landing checklist," I say. My left hand is now on the nose wheel steering bar as we follow the yellow taxi lines, turn off switches, and bring flaps up and spoilers down, cleaning up the airplane. No need to shut down an engine as we usually do to save fuel. It's already down.

"How are the brakes?" I ask.

"Hot," Jim responds, looking at the gauges on his panel. It's no wonder at this weight.

"Real hot. Number four main body is in the red." Not good. That could overheat a wheel, causing a fuse plug to blow and a tire to deflate if it works right. Or, if it doesn't work right, the tire might explode. Jim suggests we stop short of the terminal to let the brakes cool on the ramp. I agree. It should only take a few minutes more. I pick up the PA and ask the passengers for just a little more patience, please, in the name of safety, and I explain this latest situation. One of the ground agents comes out to the plane and plugs in a headset under the nose that allows us to communicate. I explain the problem and our plan. He suggests we shut down the engines and he'll get the tractor hooked up to tow us to the jetway. The wheels can be chocked and the brakes can be released to cool more quickly. Sounds good. Brakes are beginning to cool, but they are still in the red. We are almost home.

I see portable stairs drive by down below on the ramp and wonder where they are going and what is happening. Then I hear, "Welcome to Newark, folks. If you will just follow me down the stairs and across the ramp...."

I wonder what could be happening. The 485 passengers that I worked very hard to safely return to earth are about to walk right next to tires that might explode! If they would just wait another two minutes, we would have them safely at a jetway. No one will answer on the headset that's left dangling from the outlet jack. The ground agent is off looking for a tow-in tractor. I storm down the circular stairs, grab the ground agent standing at the front door by his coat sleeve and demand an explanation. His expression is my first indication of how angry I must look. He says the maintenance man told him to go get the stairs. The passengers are filing past me. No time for a friendly, "Good-bye. Hope to see you again. Have a nice day." They're probably not in the mood anyway. It's been twelve hours and two attempts, and they're back at their departure point.

I tear down the stairs and stop the maintenance truck. "Hey! What's with the stairs?"

He says, "Your wheels were chocked and engines shut down. I told them to get it ready just in case you needed them. I guess he misunderstood."

"Misunderstood?" I'm shouting. All the built-up adrenaline from the last two hours comes rushing to the surface. "So you guys just go ahead and do it without talking to me. Don't you think a conversation with the captain might have been in order? The headset is right there. Why do you think we parked here? Don't you realize the danger? I just did everything in my power to get those people on the ground safely, and then you risk putting them in danger instead of waiting two minutes? The brakes are hot. What if a tire explodes?"

"We didn't know that." He responds with a shrug. He's a nice guy. We had worked together before over broken engines and instruments. I realize part of my reaction has to do with lack of sleep and all the adrenaline coursing through my body. I walk away, but find him later to apologize.

After getting that out of my system, I return to the cockpit to make sure we complete all the checklists and logbook entries. Maintenance could call with questions. I would call them later to hear what they found. Pete and Jim are silently putting things away in the cockpit. I don't think they had seen this side of me before. I sit in the jumpseat to catch my breath after climbing three stories of stairs. We are all exhausted.

Jim stands from the flight engineer seat, ready to leave. "I hope we get to fly together again. Maybe without so much excitement." He smiles for the first time all night.

I shake his outstretched hand. "That would be great. And thanks for the help."

"Sure. You did good." He picks up his flight bag and leaves. I sit back down, shocked, and look at Pete.

"I think he finally came around," he says, smiling, as he pulls his flight bag out from beside his seat. "He had nice things to say while you were gone. And he's right. There was a lot going on tonight. Good job."

There was nothing to say in return except "thanks." In this job, the flight operations managers and chief pilots sitting behind desks often have no idea what a pilot did or didn't do. There are no pats on the back. Promotions aren't based on performance or feedback during annual reviews. They are based on seniority and the ability to pass initial and on-going training and checkrides. A pilot is trained to handle emergencies and is expected to put that training into use if the situation arises. It's just part of the job. The closest thing to reviews are feedback from fellow pilots. Those comments make up one's reputation, a pilot's most precious asset, which is carried throughout a career. A good one is hard earned and extremely difficult to get back if ever lost or questioned. Although I couldn't expect everyone to like flying with me, I did want them to respect me as a good pilot, captain, and person.

"You ready to go in?" Pete asks, standing up.

"No. I want to double-check the maintenance write-ups and get everything I need for the FAA reports. I'm glad it was you in that seat tonight. Thanks." I mean it.

"You bet. See you next time. Go get some sleep. The report can wait." He reaches down to give me a hug before leaving. Flying can be quite a bonding experience.

David, the lead flight attendant, enters as Pete is leaving. "Hey, Captain." We are good friends, but he likes calling me Captain. "Anything I can get you from below? Everybody's off the plane. We just wanted to say thanks for all the help, for letting us know what was up, and for talking to the passengers. And, especially, for getting us back safe. We were so glad it was you up here tonight."

"Thank you for that. It means a lot. Tell the rest of the crew I said 'thanks,' too. I'm fine, don't need anything else. Drive carefully going home. It's the most dangerous part of your trip," he says with a smile.

"Yes, ma'am. You take care, too." He returns the smile and gives me a hug before leaving.

I sit in the silent airplane, looking out the front window as the morning sun makes airplane-shaped shadows on the ramp three stories below. I pat the dashboard in the way I used to pat my horse's neck after a long, fast ride, thanking her for the fun, for keeping me safe, for working with me as an extension of myself.

Going through 747 captain training only six months earlier, I had wondered what it would be like if an emergency occurred out in the real world instead of in the confines of the training center and simulator. Were those nay-saying pilots right? Could a female handle an emergency on a heavy aircraft under adverse conditions? Would a male crew accept a female as their captain? How would I be received? How would I react under that level of pressure? Now I knew.

Lynn's aviation career began in 1972 as a TWA flight attendant then retired from United Airlines as a pilot in 2013. She has flown captain on the Boeing 727, B737 and B747. Captain Rippelmeyer's new passion is her charitable nonprofit called ROSE—a Roatan Support Effort. She also spends her time snorkeling and golfing.

Captain Lynn Rippelmeyer with Beverly Himmelfarb.

My First Lesson
by Suzanne Alley

I t was 1972, and I was a nineteen-year-old pre-med student at the University of Georgia.

My two roommates and I got jobs working as cocktail waitresses on the weekends at a place called The Key to America. Hank Williams Jr. played there frequently, and we made tons of tip money, maybe because we wore hot pants and high heels!

One night I waited on a table of six men who kept me really busy all night. Lots of drinks. When it came time to pay, they were counting out pennies and barely had enough money to cover the bill. They said they were very sorry, but they didn't have any more money for a tip. It must have been the look on my face that caused them to put their heads together and come up with a plan. They told me that they were all flight instructors at the Athens airport, and they had decided to give me a flying lesson as a tip.

Much to their dismay, I showed up at the airport the next day to collect. They were all feeling the effects of the previous night of partying. Finally, one of the instructors offered to take me up. I absolutely fell in love with flying that day. The man who gave me my first flying lesson was Mike Daskivich, and he became my mentor and lifelong friend.

After a few months of scrounging flying lessons, I got up the nerve to tell my parents that I wasn't going to study to be a doctor anymore. I was going to be a pilot! They responded by calling a family conference and told me I was "throwing my life away."

I saw an ad for Embry-Riddle Aeronautical University in the back of a "Flying Magazine" and decided that was where I needed to be, so I headed down to Daytona Beach. After earning my flight ratings, I instructed at New Smyrna Beach Airport in the mornings, giving multi-engine ratings in an old Apache. Days were spent in classes at ERAU, and in the afternoons I worked there as a flight instructor. Weekends were spent working at the Jai-Alai Fronton and the dog track. I ate lots of oatmeal in those days—cheap and filling. (And, I've finally made my peace with the stuff!)

After graduation, I moved back to Atlanta and flew Purolator Freight runs in the middle of the night, single pilot, in various light twins. We had no radar and no heater. I carried a 357 Magnum, as Fulton County Airport was a pretty scary place to be alone at 4:00 a.m. We had to load and unload all of the freight by ourselves. My dad called me a truck driver.

Always looking to build my credentials, I interviewed with everyone who would talk to me. One man who was in charge of hiring for the FAA (doing flight checks in a Hawker) let me interview three times before telling me, "Honey, I can't hire you. My wife would never speak to me again."

I did get a job with Planes, Inc., and spent a few years there flying freight and charter in Metroliners and Lear Jets.

In 1981, I was lucky enough to be hired by Piedmont Airlines. In 1983, I was the first officer on a Boeing 737 with Captain Cheryl Peters. We were the first all-female crew to pilot a jet for a major airline.

I've been an airline pilot for over thirty-five years now, and I still love it. It is pretty crazy to think my career began with a tip!

Suzanne was hired by Piedmont Airlines in 1981 and a week before she retired from USAir/American in May of 2018 she married. Thirty-seven years of flying and "loving every moment—it is crazy to think my career began with a tip!" Captain Alley has two fantastic adult children.

Stop Smoking
by Gail Martin

After graduation from Embry-Riddle in 1979, I went to work as a flight instructor for a fixed base operator in New Haven, Connecticut. They also had a small commuter airline called New Haven Airways. The commuter airline had multi-engine Piper aircraft, Twin Otters, and the eighteen-passenger Embraer Bandeirante turboprop. We flew to all three New York City airports, Philadelphia, Baltimore, and Washington, D.C. After building experience and flight hours, I checked out as captain in 1981.

The first day that I flew the Bandeirante as captain, with a female first officer, Regina Grisafi, we were faced with an unusual situation. We were flying from New Haven to Washington, D.C., with a full flight of businessmen and one long-haired young man. The flight deck was separated from the cabin by a curtain. About thirty minutes into the flight, we smelled what we thought were cigarettes. As our flights were non-smoking, this was a problem. I left Gina in charge and headed to the back. It was immediately apparent to me that what I smelled was marijuana smoke, not tobacco. As I looked around the cabin, I saw all the businessmen, but I did not see the young man!

This was a small airplane, so where could he be? The cabin was separated from the rear cargo area by a detachable net. As I walked towards the back of the airplane, I saw this individual in the cargo area (he had unfastened the net and walked in) smoking marijuana. I said, "What are you doing back here?" He said, "I'm looking for the bathroom." I told him, "Stop smoking, return to your seat, and do not get up again!" Then I said, "If you do not comply, I will land this plane at a small airport in the middle of nowhere and kick you off." Thankfully, he was not a problem for the rest of the flight.

Gina and I both had the same goal—to be airline pilots. We now became very worried because we were knowingly carrying a person on an airplane who has some quantity of marijuana. This is against the Federal Aviation Regulations. We were also worried that some of the businessmen would complain about secondhand marijuana smoke and its effects. We went ahead and called to have the police meet the airplane. They did, but they released the individual after finding only a tiny quantity of marijuana. We did the return flight back to New Haven and went home.

Later that night, I received a phone call. The person said he was from the FAA and that I must fly down to Washington, D.C., to meet with him tomorrow. He said that I had violated the law by knowingly landing at a federal airport with someone who had marijuana in their possession and that it didn't matter that it was only a small quantity. I was immediately upset and worried about how that would affect my future career goals, so I called my boss and told him what happened. I said I would need a day off to fly down and meet with the

FAA. Rather than reassure me that everything would be fine, he said, "This is bad news. You're really in a bad situation, and maybe you need a lawyer." He then put me on hold, saying he had to check the schedule to get me the day off.

He came back on the line with the speakerphone and a chorus of laughter. Turns out it was my co-workers who tricked me, pretending to be from the FAA. It was such a great prank on their part, I couldn't be mad! I never did hear anything about the incident from any authority.

New Haven Airways was a great place to get my flight experience, which led to a corporate flying job and the getting hired by USAir in June 1983. I have thirty-three years with the company and am currently flying as captain on the Airbus 319, 320, and 321.

How I got started in flying...

I'd always wanted to travel and see the world. Perhaps it was from looking through my father's gigantic stack of National Geographic magazines. When I was twelve years old, our local Girl Scout troop toured the United Airlines training center in the Chicago area. I was very impressed and decided I would like to become a flight attendant. I finished high school with good grades and as a member of the National Honor Society. But my father said, "Go to work. I'm not giving you a dime for college because you're just going to get married." After graduating high school in 1975, I worked in downtown Chicago as a receptionist in an office. By August, three months later, I knew this was not the life for me. I enrolled myself in a local community college and began waitressing in an effort to further my career. I still had the desire to be a flight attendant, but I worked on getting a degree in accounting as a backup.

In order to make my flight attendant application look better, I decided to take some flying lessons. I had very little money, so paying for them was stressful. However, I really did enjoy it! At the time, the earliest anyone could get hired as a flight attendant with a major airline was twenty years of age.

I put applications in everywhere and was thrilled when, two days after my twentieth birthday, I had an interview with TWA airlines. To this day, I can remember the pain of opening their rejection letter. I then asked my flight instructor, "What else can I do to work for an airline? Ticket agent? Work the ramp?" He said, "Why don't you be an airline pilot?" After all these years of thinking about the airlines, that idea had never occurred to me! I thought being a pilot was something women just didn't do. But three months later, I left Chicago with $1500 and my private license. I moved to Florida to start flight training at Embry Riddle. I decided it was going to work out somehow once I got there.

Through lots of hard work and several student loans, I graduated in 1979. I worked for New Haven Airways from 1979 to 1983. While there, I accumulated 3000 hours of flight time, many of those hours as captain in twin-engine turbo props. In January 1983, I was hired by General Foods Corporation as a copilot on their Falcon business jet. While that was a great job, I could not resist the lure of the airlines. When USAir called in June 1983—I was twenty-six—I decided to take the position. My first duty there was as a flight engineer on a 727. It was difficult to learn the 727 airplane systems. Hydraulics? Air conditioning packs? But sitting sideways was a good place to start at the airline. Most men did not want women in the flight deck, but they weren't checked out on "the panel" and had to rely on us. After that, I flew the BAC-111, DC-9, MD-80 as first officer, and the BAE-146, B737, and Airbus 319, 320, and 321 as captain. In spite of airline bankruptcies—and the loss of my pension—I've still had a wonderful career. I feel proud to be able to get people where they need to go in a safe and efficient manner. I especially love seeing people reunited with their families at the baggage claim area!

Gail began her career in 1979 flying for New Haven Airways. She is currently in her thirty-fifth year with American Airlines; twenty-nine years as a captain. Captain Martin is looking forward to retiring to spend more time with her husband, children, and five grandchildren!

Mission Complete
by Lucy Young

O n August 25, 2011, I was a reserve captain out of
Charlotte Douglas International (CLT) in North
Carolina. Despite being on short call, I went out on
Lake Norman with friends in a pontoon boat. I knew I could
get to work within two hours if needed, so all was well. Sure
enough, I got called out for a three-day trip, and my friends
deposited me ashore. I headed home and then to work.

Hurricane Irene was making the news. The three-day trip
turned into a memorable one—all good. At 1530, I reported to
the crew room and met my highly experienced, super-nice first
officer, Melissa Monahan. Melissa had worked for a time at
jetBlue, then took a recall to US Airways in 2007, around the
same time that I regained my left seat bid on the Airbus 320.

Our first leg was to Bradley Field, serving Hartford,
Connecticut, and Springfield, Massachusetts. At the gate, I
learned I had an all-female crew, which is always fun, and of
course I wanted to take photos. The flight attendants were

Helen Heron, Julia Kozlova, and Mary Mann. Then, I learned there was an FAA jumpseater, who turned out to be my friend Marilyn Pearson, whom I knew from several Women Take Flight programs at the New England Air Museum. Marilyn is delightful and easy-going, making the FAA Safety Inspector "observation" flight easy, which was a relief. She was a good sport, and we got a group photo of all six of us women before boarding. The subsequent legs were back to Charlotte, then on to Chicago for the night.

August 26, 2011

The next day was a leisurely morning in Chicago, and we flew to Philadelphia and Tampa in the afternoon. Hurricane Irene was picking up steam in the Outer Banks and was expected to hit Wilmington, North Carolina, that night. I was praying for everyone there because my parents used to live in that area and I knew how devastating the hurricanes could be in coastal North Carolina. The weather channels were showing the NOAA P-3 Orion aircraft "Hurricane Hunters" flying patterns around the hurricane. This was interesting to me because I had flown in P-3s in the Navy and knew of a female Hurricane Hunter pilot when weather reconnaissance was still a Navy mission.

August 27, 2011

On day three we reported to the Tampa International Airport early to fly to Washington, D.C. A very nicely dressed professional-looking woman in the TSA security line looked at me with a don't-I-know-you-from-somewhere expression.

It turned out to be Dr. Kathryn Sullivan, a Navy mission specialist astronaut who was now the Deputy Administrator for NOAA. She was one of the first six women selected as a NASA astronaut and the first woman to walk in space. I had met her at a Women in Aviation conference and through Navy friends. She was a naval reserve oceanographer and held the rank of captain. It was great to have her on board, and I quickly requested a first class seat for her and her aide and let them board early. She had just flown on the NOAA P-3s that I had seen depicted on TV. She was on her way to Washington to report to the NOAA command center because Irene was barreling up the coast toward the Delmarva Peninsula and she needed to be at the nerve center of the operation. It was so interesting to hear her describe these missions.

As we landed in Washington, the winds were picking up and it was raining steadily. Flight operations would not be going on much longer in the area. We refueled, loaded up, and headed back to Charlotte before the storm hit.

Hurricane Irene was the seventh costliest hurricane in American history, with 56 deaths and a price tag of 15.6 billion dollars. Mission complete!

Lucy became a naval aviator in 1977 and flew the Douglas TA-4 Skyhawk, then McDonnell Douglas C-9 transports in Operation Desert Shield/Storm. She now flies the Airbus for American Airlines. Captain Young enjoys hiking in national parks and visiting friends all over the world.

Between the Sun and Antarctica
by Davida Forshaw

D eparture time had come and gone. Our fully-laden aircraft, a VH-OEI, was still attached to the aerobridge at the extremity of the Melbourne Airport domestic terminal. It was the only gate that could accommodate the reach of the two hundred and thirteen-foot wingspan of the Boeing 747-400ER Longreach aircraft, in a terminal set up for the smaller members of the Qantas fleet. All Qantas B747-400 aircraft carry the word Longreach as part of their nomenclature to recognize the Queensland town where Qantas (Queensland and Northern Territory Aerial Services) first started operations in 1920, and also as a nod to the aircraft's incredible range and size. For the airport staff, the domestic terminal provided many logistical challenges on the rare occasions it was required to accommodate one.

Today, though, we had another problem. No matter how much we sharpened our pencils we could not make the aircraft's takeoff performance figures work. For the last day of the year, Melbourne had turned on what we Down Unders call "a scorcher." It was a record temperature of 42.9 degrees Celsius (109.22° Fahrenheit) at 1715 hours. The previous record of 41.7 degrees Celsius for December 31st was set back in 1862. It was hot, too hot for our four General Electric engines to develop enough thrust for takeoff.

The Boeing 747-400 aircraft is the love of my life. From the first time I had the privilege to fly her, I knew we were a perfect match. To this day I am still captivated by the beauty and elegance of the aircraft if I happen to see one in flight. The versatility and range of the aircraft is exceptional. The 747 can takeoff and, up to fourteen hours later, deliver four hundred people to where they wanted to go. However, I had never flown one like this before, as a joy flight zigzagging around the southern continent at 18,000 feet.

The original plan was to depart Melbourne in the late afternoon, fly south over Tasmania and the Southern Ocean, and into the perpetual light of the Antarctic Circle. It takes three hours flight time to reach the circle and one more hour till we are overhead the frozen continent. Then we would meander around Antarctica, providing a once in a lifetime sightseeing tour for four hours in perfect daylight. There our passengers would celebrate New Year's Eve with champagne, fine food, and dazzling views. Time was of the essence.

We had started our preparations two days before at a briefing in Qantas' flight training centre in Melbourne. The flight crew was to become qualified in "Ice and Polar Emergency Procedures," as our normal annual emergency procedures training was not sufficient to cover this extreme operation. Our training included the fitting and wearing of polar suits, polar gloves, and goggles. Surviving in polar temperatures requires minimizing the exposure of the skin to the elements by wearing all available clothing and positioning survivors in sheltered areas out of the icy winds; sunglasses and snow goggles must also be worn to prevent snow blindness. The cumbersome gloves are to prevent frostbite and skin damage, but try doing anything while wearing them! We practiced picking up survival beacons and first aid kits with them on. Our instructor talked about looking through the aircraft to salvage any equipment that could be used to help survive in the ice and snow. Of course, blankets, pillows, and seat cushions are obvious items to take, but even the aircraft carpets, curtains, and seat-belt webbing can be used to erect shelters. It was all very fascinating in theory.

By 1800 hours we were locked up, ready to go. We had all our passengers, crew, Antarctic specialists, and even a four-piece roving jazz band on board. We were literally sweating for the outside air temperature to drop by a minimum of 2°C (3.5°F) to get under our critical takeoff temperature limit. Sitting at our maximum takeoff weight of 412,769 kilograms (910,000 pounds), we were between a rock and a hard place. If we took off fuel to decrease the aircraft's takeoff weight, we would have to reduce the sightseeing time for flying over Antarctica. Taking off passengers was out of the question! Thirty minutes later it finally happened. The new aerodrome information was released with a temperature of 40°C (104°F) and we were back in business.

The mood on the aircraft was festive. Champagne was popping in the cabin and the crew was setting up for the dinner service. In the flight deck, despite hearing the wafting notes of the jazz music from our roving band, we were all business. Once the cruise was established, we instigated a satellite telephone call with our Australian meteorologists in Antarctica to confirm where the skies were clear. Cloud cover would interfere with our sightseeing plans, so we wanted to know where the clearest skies over the icy continent were so we could fly straight there and give our passengers the best views possible. The meteorology scientists at Davis, our most southerly Australian Antarctic station, wanted to get back to us after they received the next satellite sweep images. It would be another thirty minutes till they could give us the latest information so we could make a definitive flight plan. We just decided to keep our southerly track until then.

We turned our attention to the rarely used 'Heading Reference Switch' on the centre panel of the flight deck. This switch usually sits in the 'NORM' position, referencing magnetic north; in fact, I had never seen it in any other position except during my ground-training course! However, once south of latitude 60°S in the Antarctic Circle, we had to position the switch to 'TRUE' to reference True North for our primary flight displays and navigation displays. We cannot reference the magnetic compass in the Antarctic Circle, as the difference between the south magnetic pole and the south geographic pole is approximately 1543 nautical miles. It was a big moment for the flight deck crew, as we rarely fly that far south. Finally we received another satellite call from Davis base to confirm the areas of cloud cover and the areas that were best to head for the views, and the plan was confirmed.

I left the flight deck and went back into the business class cabin on my first break. The jazz band was in full swing, roaming the aisles. Main course had been served, and all the passengers I spoke with were looking forward to seeing the amazing views of Antarctica. There was one beautiful couple celebrating their 40th wedding anniversary. As we spoke, they told me they had brought their whole family, a party of ten, including children and grandchildren, for a night to remember in the family memoirs.

Half an hour before we crossed the coastline of the southern continent, we set up another satellite telephone call with

Davis. This time we patched the call into the PA system and had one of our Antarctic experts interview the Davis scientists about life on the base. Their enthusiasm for the groundbreaking research work they were conducting was evident as they told us what a normal day in the life of an Antarctic scientist entailed. It was also evident that they felt privileged to be part of the specialist team for the summer's work. The professional tone of the discourse belied the fact that they were excited to have contact with real people from the outside world.

It was determined by the last satellite sweep that the clearest views would be in the McMurdo Sound and Ross Island region. We crossed the coast at Cape North jutting out into the Ross Sea and flew towards the Sound, descending the aircraft to our lowest safe altitude. Antarctica is the highest of all the continents with an average elevation of 8200 feet (2500m).

Mount Erebus, the southern most active volcano on earth, rose ahead of us, spouting ash and sulphuric smoke from its core. It was a most unusual sight rising above the expanse of snow. The flight crew paused to remember the day in 1979 when the fateful flight of Air New Zealand Flight 901 had impacted the side of the mountain. There had been a discrepancy between the authorized flight plan and the positions given to the crew to be loaded into the inertial navigation system of the DC-10. This should have resulted in the aircraft being positioned 43 kilometres (27 miles) to the west of the 12,448 foot (3794m) Mt. Erebus, flying along the coast of McMurdo Sound. Our hearts went out to the families of the crew and passengers of that flight who to this day are affected by the tragedy. It was also a stark reminder of the harsh realities of such a beautiful place on earth.

We kept a very strict discipline in the flight deck as we banked the aircraft left, then right. Qantas has been conducting these flights for many years, and we adhered to a strict set of specialized procedures. We had four pilots on the flight deck at all times over the continent. At any time, two of us were flying the aircraft, plotting our track, and scanning the instruments, while the other two were looking outside, confirming our position the old-fashioned way, map to ground. Every thirty minutes we would swap positions.

Many assume that the ground in Antarctica is completely covered in ice and snow, but I was to learn that this is not true. There is a region known as the Dry Valleys, so named because of their lack of snow or ice cover. The Antarctic specialist explained as we flew over them that the nearby mountains are so high that the seaward flowing ice is blocked from reaching the Ross Sea, leaving the valley floor covered with dry, loose gravel. There is also a roaring wind in this region, caused by the cold dense air being pulled down the side of the mountains by gravity. It picks up to speeds of 320kph (200mph) into the valleys and heats as it descends, resulting in the melting of any ice or snow. This unique phenomenon gave rise to some spectacular views and many clicks of the camera shutters throughout the aircraft.

It was approaching midnight on New Year's Eve and the jazz band had started up again in preparation for the countdown. More champagne was flowing in the cabin. The New Year was celebrated whilst flying over the American McMurdo Base and nearby New Zealand Scott Station, situated on Ross Island. We could clearly see the buildings and huts that make up the research stations beneath the midnight sun.

Of course the timing of midnight on New Year's Eve is all relative. You really can choose any time you like, as Antarctica sits on every line of longitude and the continent has no official time zone. The convention, however, is for the research bases to synchronize with their home country or their main supply base. Who were we to go against convention? After two more spectacular hours of twisting and weaving over the ever-changing landscape, we celebrated New Year's Eve for the second time, with another round of Auld Lang Syne, as most of our sightseeing had occurred over New Zealand territory.

The bittersweet time had arrived, and we began to plan our return journey to Melbourne. We had been mindful throughout the flight of our latest return time the further south we journeyed. Engine failure and depressurization diversion scenarios can become critical very quickly in such a remote region. These positions had been calculated before departure, but the crew constantly reviewed them in light of the flexible flight plan. In the last half hour we had slowly made our way back north along McMurdo Sound to Cape Adare where the skies had been clear. It was now time to leave the continent behind and head back towards the Antarctic Circle.

Crossing Latitude 60°S, we noticed the midnight sun slowly dip below the horizon, and a twilight set in for the final three hours of our journey. Inside the cabin reflected our new outside conditions, as the buzzing hum diminished and the passengers settled down for a few hours of sleep before our dawn arrival home.

At Qantas we have a tradition of naming our Boeing 747-400 Longreach aircraft after Australia's major cities or towns. VH-OEI is so named "Ceduna" after a major fishing port on the southern coast of the state of South Australia. Ceduna is a derivative of the Aboriginal word Chedoona, meaning "a place to sit down and rest." And this is precisely what I have done many times as I reflected on how privileged I was to be part of this aeronautical adventure: to fly my beloved B747 to the limits of its capability and to have seen the beauty of Antarctica with my own eyes.

Davida has been with Qantas Airways for seventeen years and is currently flying the Boeing 787-900. A strong advocate for guiding young women into STEM opportunities, Davida is also enjoying long distance running, traveling with her family, and cuddling Hercules—her Russian Blue cat!

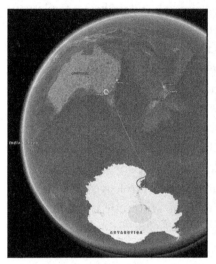

Don't Talk on the Radio!
by Karlene Petitt

The year was 1996, and the airline—Tower Air. I was employed as a Boeing 747 first officer, skipping the entry level of a second officer, because Tower operated with professional flight engineers. Not only did I jump into the right seat, I was also the first female pilot at Tower Air. Management's only concerns revolved around my being a woman and where I was about to fly.

Tower spooled up hiring around November/December to prepare to fly the Hadj—the Muslim pilgrimage to Mecca. Challenges were many on these flights, from attempted cooking in the aisles with Bunsen burners, to death. Not death by cooking—thankfully the flight attendants put the fires out, but death because some Muslims waited too long to make the required holy journey and passed before they arrived. If they could die on the aircraft upon their return, then life ended perfectly, as it should. Except for the flight crew dealing with logistics.

The challenge would be flying this Middle East assignment as a woman. Women were not readily accepted as professionals, thus to have one flying the aircraft? Oh—God forbid. When the religious police pulled over a crew van, the women were expected to be sitting in the far back, never in front. What would they do with a female in the front of the aircraft? Thankfully cloaked guardians never wandered the tarmac.

Tower Air management warned me to be careful and gave me a few survival tips.

"They don't want you there."

"You might be targeted."

"Don't talk on the radio."

"Don't remove your jacket."

"Don't go into flight operations."

This mission was more than ominous. I would be traveling to the other side of the world, a place that I would not be wanted or accepted. However, flying a Boeing 747 this early in my career was a great opportunity. Thus, I accepted my new job and flew through training without a hitch. I can't take the credit—Tower had some exceptional instructors, and I had a strong foundation from Captain Bo Corby, who taught me how to fly a jet while I was a low time propeller pilot. Lesson learned: Be grateful for those teachers in your life.

Operational experience—O.E.—was a round trip from New York to Miami, and then I was complete—so far so good. The next trip would be an L.A. turn, and then I would be destined for the Middle East.

I Don't Want You Here

Looking forward to my LAX flight I arrived early, checked the paperwork, and prepared for our flight. Then the captain arrived. I said hello, which was returned with some guttural sound. I shrugged, and then stood quietly while he repeated the efforts I had just gone through in preparation, clearly not interested in my input. Then we headed to the aircraft.

The captain walked quickly across the ramp to keep one step ahead of me. Then halfway to the aircraft he stopped walking. He may have become exhausted because he stood much shorter than I, and his little legs were walking as quickly as possible to stay in front. But when he stopped, he turned, dropped his bags and pointed a finger at me. "I don't want you here!" he spat.

What response do you give to a statement like that? "Thank you for being honest?" I wasn't wanted, and this guy turned out to be a chief pilot. He started as a mechanic, became a flight engineer, and then earned his pilot certificate. Thus, Tower gave this non-experienced pilot a chance. Time and moving to the left seat, and multiple chief pilots quitting (four that year) found him in the chief pilot's office with an attitude: I got mine, now the ladder comes up.

"Holy crap. In the United States of America. And they warned me about attitudes in Saudi Arabia?" Seriously?

You Might be Targeted

Two months later I found myself standing in a souk, an open-air market, in Saudi Arabia with my captain. We had wandered around checking out shops and ended up in a jewelry store. I had never seen so many jewels. A particular diamond and emerald necklace stood out and was valued at $250,000. The salesman held it out, and said, "You try. Take outside and see how beautiful." Holding up both hands, I firmly said, "No thank you."

The man was insistent. "Please. Will be so beautiful. Please take look in sunshine." He attempted to shove the jewels into my hands. Something felt wrong. "I looked him in the eye and said, "No. Thank you," pushing them back. I probably should have put my hands behind my back. However, I simply thought that he trusted me. People didn't steal, or their hands would be cut off, so he wasn't worried. I later learned from our liaison that the shopkeeper was setting me up. Had I gone outside he would have yelled, "Thief!" and I would have been imprisoned. Not only would I have been imprisoned, but I would have received no food, water, or been allowed a phone call.

Later that day in the souk, during prayer time when all the shops were closed, my captain and I were sitting on a bench. The religious police approached—a large man in a robe, with two armed police at each side. He said to the captain sitting beside me, "Cover your head!" The captain tried to explain that I would cover my head, when the shops opened. He said again, "Cover your head." He wouldn't look at me, but he was clearly telling the man sitting next to me to manage his woman. The captain attempted to explain I would cover my head when we could buy something. This non-communication went back and forth a couple times. I finally spoke. "When the stores open I will get something to cover my head." Not original, but effective. His eyes flashed to me, I smiled, and then he glared at the captain and said, one more time (to him), "Cover your head." He turned and walked away. There are many things I could say about being a 'nothing' in the eyes of a culture. However, when a man gets yelled at for my behavior? Hmm, perhaps we should adopt that part of the culture in the western world.

Don't Talk on the Radio

The company thought that keeping me hidden, and not speaking on the radio, would help hide the fact a woman was operating the aircraft. The week had been long, we were all tired and we had a long day ahead of us. All we wanted to do was get out of town. The captain called for pushback clearance since I wasn't allowed to talk on the radio. Then ATC proceeded to allow everyone else to push who called after us. I finally said, "Let me have a try." I called and requested a pushback clearance. We received an immediate clearance. That was the day we learned if we wanted to get out Mecca, let the woman talk on the radio, as they did everything to allow us to leave first. The power of being an unwanted woman—expedited clearances.

A few weeks later I was in the terminal and a Saudi pilot walked up and said, "Are you the woman we are hearing on the radio?" I said, "Yes." He extended his hand with a huge smile and said, "Nice to see it." Most definitely—that was nice to see.

Don't Remove Your Jacket

Not removing my uniform jacket didn't sound so bad—until I was sitting in a broken plane for an hour in Istanbul, without an APU. The APU is an auxiliary power unit that provided air conditioning. Without it we were more than melting, we were boiling. I then had to put my jacket on to walk across the ramp in 114-degree Fahrenheit temps from the broken plane to another aircraft. I felt as if I would pass out. Thirty seconds into my walk, I removed my jacket, in front of God and everyone. I remember standing there for a moment. I looked up, and then over my shoulder and across the ramp. The sky did not fall, and the wrath of Allah did not come down upon me.

I did however wear my jacket through the terminal, and all other times I didn't feel as if I were going to pass out due to heatstroke. One day as I followed the guys through security, there was a man patting down the pilots. I stepped through and he started at my feet, up my legs, over torso and up to my—Oh my. He quickly removed his hands from my body, and his eyes widened as he looked up at my face. Everyone standing by froze. Silence prevailed. The poor man, I thought he was going to die. Actually, he probably did, too. Seriously, he had a high chance of death for touching a woman in public. My reaction: I laughed. Chuckled really, more out of embarrassment than anything. Then instantly everyone relaxed, one of the guards nodded my way, and I returned the nod. From then on, every time I approached security, the officer tapped the edge of his arm, as if acknowledging my stripes, and they allowed me to pass.

Don't Go into Flight Operations

I had been warned that flight operations in Saudi was off limits to women—this was a man's world. I had to stand in the terminal and wait for the men to preflight. One day a new captain said, "Come on, let's go preflight." I explained my orders. He said with a big grin, "Let's go change a little culture." We went inside, and eyes widened, whispers ensued, but nothing happened. I just smiled at everyone and did my job. Another hurdle, and the world did not end.

Checklist Complete

I thought everything I had been warned about had been addressed. Yet, nobody told me what to do when a manager of Saudi Airlines brought me gifts. Well, I probably should not have taken a beautifully giftwrapped package (unopened) through security, and onto the airplane. That was something we didn't think of back then but know better today. While we waited in a long taxi line, I opened up the gift and it was a beautiful white silk abaya—a robe.

My flight engineer told me I was never getting my exit visa and that I would be wife number nine. Okay. Up until this point, the gifts were only chocolate and assorted treats. Thus, upon returning I asked the liaison for his advice about accepting gifts. He said, "Just keep them. It means nothing, but you don't want to offend him giving them back." A week later I received a dozen red roses with a card stating, "I wish I could give you the entire garden."

When I entered the lobby to pick up my roses, he was waiting. We sat in the coffee shop and talked. It turned out that he had only one wife, and she wanted to work. He could not understand why his wife wanted to work, because she would spend all her earned money on childcare. Two days later I had my exit visa and left town early...without telling my admirer of my early departure.

The Gift of Flight

The world is filled with unique cultures and attitudes. You can walk across the ramp in New York at JFK and receive an archaic opinion of not belonging because you're a woman; or you can be sitting on the other side of the world with a man who doesn't understand why his wife wants to work. Which country is which?

Flying in the Middle East was an experience I will never forget. Tower Air was one of eight airlines that I have flown with, and each airline has provided an exceptional experience. This adventure reminds me that when we find the courage to take that step forward into an unknown and fearful world, we make a difference, albeit small at times, paving the way for pilots who follow in our contrails. ISA pilots extend a helping hand for those who come behind to achieve all they can be, knowing they will be leading future generations. We share our experiences for all to enjoy. And we always talk on the radio.

Karlene's thirty-eight-year career includes eight airlines, seven Boeing type-ratings, an Airbus 330 type, and twenty-one years instructing. She currently flies the Boeing 777 for Delta, is an author, speaker, and a Doctoral Candidate at Embry-Riddle Aeronautical University promoting aviation safety. http://karlenepetitt.blogspot.com/

Karlene with WASP Dawn Seymour at Dawn's 100th birthday party at Women in Aviation four months before she passed away.

Lightning Strike!
by Brenda Robinette

The year is 2010, and it's springtime in Florida. We are all too aware of what thunderstorms mean to pilots. Avoid at all costs, right? Well, after flying for twenty-five years, I finally got hit by lightning while climbing out of 16,000 feet from Tampa in a Boeing 737-700. After the shock, glowing cockpit instruments, and craziness, we flew to our destination and I grounded the airplane. It was out for repair for a few days.

That night at the hotel my hand began to hurt. It was a sharp burning pain with aching. I wrapped it up in a warm towel and that helped a little. A few days later, some small robin's egg-looking-shaped knots appeared under my skin on my left hand. I had been perfectly fine till the lightning strike, so I began to worry a bit. About every three days, something else would happen. Whatever was going on in my body was moving around. My other hand, then my jaw, then my shoulder. Finally, my left foot hurt so much that at times I couldn't even walk.

I saw a nerve specialist in May, but he found no damage and referred me to a rheumatologist. I thought, no way, arthritis? Well, come to find out an environmental stressor can bring on cancers, arthritis, autoimmune diseases—all kinds of things. Apparently the lightning strike triggered the RA (rheumatoid arthritis.) After seeing many specialists at some of the best hospitals, trying a holistic approach, and eating better, I still have to take medicine and injections weekly to help with the inflammation. I'm on less medication than before after taking the advice of my friend, Becky Howell, about alternative approaches I could try, like the essential oils which I use every day.

Dealing with the FAA was not much fun, but I was granted a waiver to fly after three months. Working with the FAA has taught me a lot on how to find information about what medications you can and can't fly with. I even had a very nice FAA doctor call me and interview me over the phone so I would not have to fill out fifty-three pages of questions. I currently have a six-year waiver to fly with RA. Always talk to your union doctors first. They know the ins and outs and fastest ways to get a waiver and get you back in the air.

This was 2010, then I had foot surgery in March of 2012 to remove a rheumatoid nodule. I had the surgery right after the Women in Aviation Conference so I could heal enough to make it to ISA+21 in Seattle! This was really my plan. It was a great plan, and it worked out very well until the Savor Seattle Chocolate Tour, when some tenderness started in my foot. Not to worry! My friend Kathy McCullough and I walked up several hills and bought the same comfortable athletic shoes. I love them. I think we have a picture of us wearing our new shoes.

I still have not tested positive for the rheumatoid factor, but the rheumatoid nodule taken out of my left foot seems to confirm the RA. Lightning can do strange things!

Brenda is celebrating her twentieth year at Southwest Airlines. Captain Robinette lives on a fifty-acre farm in Tennessee with her husband, Rob, and loves hiking, kayaking, and all outdoor activities. They also have five goats and three dogs!

Some Lessons Learned in Thirty Years of Flying

by Shannon Jipsen

I overcame my fear of flying, and now I'm a Boeing 747 captain flying all over the world. What an amazing journey!

It's a privilege, and those of us who fly for a living get to experience things that most people will only dream of seeing and doing. For those of you who are just starting out, please realize your career will literally fly by! For those of you that are nearing retirement, enjoy those last few years, as they, too, will quickly come to an end. For those of you that paved the way for those of us that followed and have already retired, thank you. Your efforts are greatly appreciated, whether it was on the line or union involvement, or just by being there and being a part of the whole. We now have a small percentage of women on flight decks all over the world. Here are a few memories and lessons I've learned along the way.

One night, flying from Ontario, CA, to Boeing Field in Seattle, WA, in a Boeing 727 we were engulfed with ribbons of the aurora. Blue, green, and white all around us—quite a sight. Another night I was flying from Louisville, KY, to Montreal, Canada, and saw a comet shooting across the sky. What beauty! With these spectacular sights, along with the majesty of the mountains as I departed Anchorage, AK, or the mountains that dot the terrain across China or the massive deserts across the Middle East to the thousands of miles of ocean that I've crossed, I'm reminded that flying is a freedom that few will experience and even fewer will understand. This career has been challenging and rewarding and, at times, frustrating, yet always fulfilling. Never forget where you started nor the people that helped you get where you are because you did not get there alone.

Take your training seriously and learn to apply it in all situations. I had a multi-engine student on his first flight in a Beechcraft Duchess. We experienced a problem with the left main landing gear. After doing everything the book said to do and doing all I could think of, I reached out to our mechanic, and they called Beechcraft for input. We never did get the gear down, so I ended up having to do a gear-up landing. This was all before I had even had Crew Resource Management (CRM) training, but I utilized what I had been taught and the things I had picked up along my flying journey at that point, and we had a successful outcome. Very little damage was done to the aircraft and we walked away safely. Due to a manufacturing defect in the left main gear spar, it broke, and we got stuck dealing with it. That's part of life as a pilot. Remember to always utilize ALL sources of input (if there's time) when dealing with a problem.

During one situation years ago, I was a B-727 Flight Engineer Initial Operating Experience Instructor and had a gateway manager blame me for a delay. Although this was not true and I had to defend myself and my student, I had a captain who stood by me and showed me true leadership skills in how to work with people that only want to blame rather than fix the problem. Part of being a good captain is to back and support your crew.

One morning going into Jacksonville, FL, I was the flight engineer on a B-727. The captain and first officer were great guys that I had flown with before. The weather was marginal, and we were cleared for the Instrument Landing System approach. The captain wasn't fully established, yet he started down. I spoke up and said we should go around. There was no response. A few seconds later, I said it again and, just as I was about to push the throttles up myself, he executed the go-around. The next night, the captain apologized to the first officer and me for putting us in that situation. He hadn't realized how tired he was and had made a bad decision. He thanked me for being persistent and doing the right thing. That lesson taught me to always speak up and, when I would become a captain, to always listen to my other crewmembers. It was a good CRM lesson! Part of being a good first officer or international relief officer (IRO) is to realize the captain may be responsible for the aircraft but that all members of the crew are critical for the safe movement of the aircraft. Never be afraid to speak up and communicate information you may have that will make a difference in the decision the captain makes.

Fatigue is frequently a problem for pilots. In my more than 27 years as an airline pilot for a cargo company, it was even more of an issue. Body clock flipping and circadian rhythm disruption wreak havoc with our bodies! Don't ever be afraid to call in fatigued if you are too tired to fly. It doesn't matter what reports you have to fill out or how much pay you could be docked. If you are tired, do not fly. It's not worth it. Your life and the lives of your crew and others are significant! I've lost friends due to fatigue. Always listen to your body. The issue of cumulative fatigue is very real. Just because you have a couple of weeks off does not mean your body is rested. The years upon years of doing this job are very hard on the body. If you are feeling the effects of cumulative fatigue, don't just brush it off. There is a learning curve to mitigate the results of fatigue. Each person is different and how it affects you depends on you. Learn what works for you: by staying hydrated, eating right, stretching and/or exercising, and sleeping as much as you can are all helpful. Still, I know my body has definitely been affected after all these years of circadian rhythm that some pilots call "flipping."

I spent fifteen years with our pilot association doing safety, accident investigation, and being a liaison between cargo carriers and Aircraft Rescue and Fire Fighting (ARFF). There are many discrepancies between passenger and cargo carriers.

Numerous regulations leave out cargo pilots and planes. Traffic Collision Avoidance System (TCAS) is one example. We had to fight for many years to get TCAS on cargo planes. Part 139, which deals with ARFF requirements, does not include cargo planes and crews. I worked for ten years to get the legislation changed, and although it has yet to be changed, there's definitely more awareness of the issue. Lithium batteries are something that we all have to deal with, but there are many issues with carrying them. There is still much work to be done for there to be "One Level of Safety" for all carriers and crews.

On a flight from Louisville to Memphis, on an Airbus 300 one night, we had a brake drag on takeoff, and we ended up with hot brakes. We left the gear down and talked to the ARFF Chief on the discrete emergency frequency (DEF) prior to landing. We made a plan to have ARFF at the approach end of the runway and had them use their Forward Looking Infra-Red (FLIR) camera to check the left main gear before we taxied in, just to be sure we didn't have any hot spots and to make sure we actually had a tire. It all worked out. We touched down with no problem and the ARFF responders checked our left main and it was okay and we taxied in with no issue. It was so good to have those guys there and available! Utilize them as a resource—they want to help if they can.

On a flight on a B-747 flying from Cologne, Germany to Hong Kong, we had many issues come up and had to get our dispatcher involved. It's a long story, but the outcome was that we had to divert at the end of a very long flight, get fuel, and fly to the original destination. My crew and I worked through the issues, made decisions together, and we safely moved the airplane. CRM skills were important that flight and, once again, I was reminded how important input is from all crewmembers and outside sources. This brings up the issue of domestic versus international operations too. Remember when you are operating outside the USA, things are different. If you've never operated outside the USA, it takes time to understand the language barriers and ways of operating in others' airspace. Learning International Civil Aviation Organization (ICAO) standards is critical and will help you transition to this arena.

On another flight, we had a situation arise that required us to divert to Taipei, Taiwan, after a very long flight day. Our dispatcher informed us that we would have to declare an emergency to land. This was very stressful, as we were getting low on fuel. We were able to make it to TPE without having to declare the emergency, but it took all of us to work together to get the airplane on the ground safely. Once again, the roles of captain, first officer, and IRO came into play during this flight. Each crewmember had a very important role in the successful outcome. As a captain, it's so very important to utilize all resources for information in the decision-making process. Realize you will never know it all and that you need your crew to assist you. Include them in everything from the paperwork review and weather observation to communicating with the company. Standard operating procedures are critical for all crewmembers to follow. Knowing the Aircraft Operations Manual (AOM) and Flight Operations Manual (FOM) is so very important for all crewmembers. When you know these books inside and out, it really does help the captain when stressful situations arise. Work together and communicate. Keep each other in the loop as to what is going on and verbalize what you need. We are human and we make mistakes, but learning to work together is critical when things aren't going "normal" in the cockpit. When we completed this flight, we debriefed on the way to the hotel. Then, we each wrote up our version of what happened and reviewed it again after we had some sleep and before I wrote a final report to be submitted to the company. As a captain it's crucial to have your first officer and IRO's perspectives in the report. My crew and I learned a lot that day.

I could go on and on, but I'll say that after all these years and thousands of hours flying around the globe, I'm thankful I got over my fear of flying and became a pilot. It has been a joy to see how the challenges have helped me grow as a person and as a professional pilot. I love being a B-747 captain. I've been so blessed.

Shannon was hired by UPS in 1991 as a Boeing 727 flight engineer. Currently she is flying the Boeing 747 and is based in Anchorage. Captain Jipsen overcame her fear of flying by learning to fly and takes pleasure in sharing her story by writing books and speaking.

Captain Shannon Jipsen with Copilot Michelle Booth.

Recollections
by Karen Kahn

Simple Pilot Math

At the beginning of my airline career in 1977, my visibility to the passengers was increased not only by my being seated at the second officer's panel next to the cockpit door, which was mostly open during passenger boarding, but also by the fact that one of my duties was to perform the pre-flight aircraft walk-around inspection.

Once complete, a favorite remark we'd often make to the flight attendants as we returned to the cockpit, particularly if one of them was new, was to tell them that part of our official airplane preflight consisted of counting the number of engines (3), multiplying by the number of wings (hopefully 2) to arrive at the number of tires (6) we should have installed. Or, to be different, we could divide the number of tires by the number of engines to get the grand total of wings. I always wanted to walk back into the aircraft, while passengers were boarding, and mumble loudly to myself, "Let's see, was that two engines and three wings or three engines and two wings?" But I suspect some travelers—and some flight attendants—might not have appreciated my humor!

Kaboom at FL 350

Most of the flights throughout my career were routine, and thankfully so. The old adage that flying is "hours of boredom punctuated by moments of sheer terror" certainly came true, though, one afternoon as we cruised high above the seemingly endless West Texas flatlands below us. We were en route from Houston to Los Angeles on the 4th of July and were not expecting any fireworks.

The flight was full. We had one hundred forty-four passengers, plus four flight attendants, two pilots, and an FAA Air Traffic Controller occupying the cockpit jumpseat. After leveling off at 35,000 feet, we began to relax for the three-hour journey ahead. I was just about to give the passengers my "Welcome Aboard from the Flightdeck" PA speech with information about the en route flight time and weather in Los Angeles, when suddenly we heard a tremendous KABOOM!

We quickly scanned the instruments, both those easily visible on the dashboard panel in front of us and those on the massive overhead ceiling panel which was extended in a 3-foot by 4-foot array of gauges, switches, knobs, and buttons above our heads. There were almost one hundred small annunciator lights on that panel and not one of them was lit up to help us identify the problem. Cabin pressurization was okay, no door lights illuminated, and the engines were running smoothly. So the first fears of a possible rapid pressurization or engine failure were quickly dispelled. The first officer wisely reached up and turned off the power to the galleys. After checking all the instruments carefully, we found nothing abnormal, but we knew there had to be something we were missing. That horrendous noise could not have meant anything but trouble.

Moments later we received a call on the cockpit-to-cabin interphone from one of our flight attendants. Mystery solved: the head flight attendant informed us that the escape slide on the forward galley door had inflated in flight, its ripcord becoming tangled in one of the rolling meal cart's wheels as they attempted to extract it from its stowage area near the 1R galley door. The noise we'd heard was the slide inflating, filling the galley area with yellow rubber, and pinning two flight attendants to the walls.

I was relieved to hear that no one was hurt. Then came the problem: how to deflate the slide so they could get on with their meal service. I suggested they use the blunt end of a knife on the valve stem if they could find it. Barring that, I told them to stab it with the knife, but watch out for another explosion!

Unfortunately, we were unable to assist with the deflation process as we were trapped in the cockpit. Inside, our jumpseat and its rider filled the cockpit doorway (it being a folding seat and he being a large man) and outside, the head flight attendant was pinned to the cockpit door by the inflated slide. He, too, was unable to help with the cleanup. Several minutes later we received an "all deflated" call, after which I managed to get back to the galley to survey the damage.

There it lay, a puddle of yellow rubber, the loudest sound I'd ever heard in my fifteen years of airline flying. (Five years later, I'd hear the sound of two main gear tires exploding on takeoff at approximately 180 mph as we left Las Vegas on a balmy April morning in 1997—but that is another story.)

Later in the flight, once we were within range of our destination, I called our Los Angeles maintenance crew and, in addition to the usual estimate of our arrival time and notes of passenger assistance needed, I mentioned the need for a new door slide. Thinking the problem was the usual one of the whole slide package becoming partly detached from the door (which occurred occasionally), they humored us by saying they'd send a mechanic to reattach the slide to the door. "No," I said, "that's not quite the problem. The slide inflated in flight, so we'll need a whole new slide, package and all."

Silence followed.

I think it was a first for them—and hopefully a last for me.

Learn from the Mistakes of Others

You'll never live long enough to make them all yourself!

That's the watchword for aviation. As an airline captain, I read all the accident reports trying to absorb the pertinent details for use in flight and on the ground. I even keep a list of "gotchas" to remind me, in the heat of battle, to pay attention to seemingly small details that can lead to disaster.

I recall an eye-opening incident during my career when my clumsiness caused some real havoc. This incident made me remember all too clearly the tragedy which resulted from a spilled cup of coffee on the instrument pedestal (*Fate is the Hunter* by Ernie Gann), when I fumbled my water bottle and squirted liquid over a panel that controls our electronic map display. It made a mess of my screen, crowding the display with unwanted GPS fixes as we descended into the Los Angeles metro area. Upon landing I called our maintenance techs and "fessed up," describing my faux pas and the type of liquid involved. It turns out that water was okay, as a hair dryer would dry it, and the instruments would recover. Soda or coffee, on the other hand, was not okay, as those would leave a residue which mandated the equipment be replaced.

More recently, I asked for more fuel before a particular flight and, fifteen minutes later, realized I'd read the flight plan wrong, mistaking one number for another. I quickly cancelled my request for additional fuel, saving everyone time, money, and hassles.

As a Critical Incident Response Program (CIRP) volunteer, I've heard many stories that crowd my brain whenever a similar situation arises, from not ensuring that the push tug is well clear of the airplane before we begin to taxi to ignoring a little "pop" noise from a circuit breaker.

Mess up? 'Fess up. That's the corollary to "learn from the mistakes of others." Hiding mistakes can be deadly and, given the immense amount of brownie points we get from admitting them, there's no reason not to use them as learning tools. Mistakes can be your best friends if you'll learn quickly from them and use the knowledge wisely in the future.

Karen was hired by Continental Airlines in July of 1977 and retired as a captain on the Boeing 757/767 in 2014. Captain Kahn enjoys her home town of Santa Barbara, traveling the world and flying "Sweet Pea," her 1975 B55 Baron. http://captainkarenkahn.com/

Passenger Reactions
by Deborah Lawrie

There have been many stories over the years about passenger reactions to female pilots and all-female flight crews. Back in the early '70s when female airline pilots were extremely few and far between, passenger reactions of shock, disbelief, amazement, curiosity, suspicion, uncertainty, and sometimes fear were common. There are many more of us today, but percentage-wise, we are still a small group. Some passengers come on board in this day and age who have never experienced a flight with a female pilot. Sometimes these uninitiated passengers still react in strange ways when they realize that one of us is at the controls.

I was the first female airline pilot in Australia after fighting a long hard battle against discrimination, which I eventually won in the High Court. Back in 1979, my legal case, known as Wardley vs. Ansett, was followed everyday by the press with newspaper articles and television reports. The court case was high profile for more than a year. As the only Australian

female in my profession, I was very conspicuous every time
I appeared anywhere in uniform. One passenger's reaction
back in the early years of my career occurred on a flight from
Melbourne to Adelaide. During cruise, the purser came to
the cockpit with a passenger's boarding pass and a request for
me to sign it. I was very flattered and pleased to see that the
boarding pass belonged to one of our male passengers.

Several years later, after an industry-changing pilot dis-
pute, I relocated to Europe and started flying with KLM
Cityhopper. It was when I was a captain on a Fokker 50 flying
the Amsterdam to Bristol and Cardiff triangle route, that one
of my most memorable passenger reaction events occurred.
There were a small number of female pilots in KLM Cityhopper
at the time, but what distinguished me from the others was
my very Australian accent. My role as captain and my accent
made this story memorable.

For me it was just another day at the office. We did not have
any technical issues and did not have much weather to worry
about. My crew consisted of a Dutch male co-pilot and two
Dutch female cabin crew. All our procedures were in English,
so there were no language issues either. We had a mixture of
mainly Dutch and English passengers on the Fokker 50, and
the first leg of the journey was from Amsterdam to Bristol.
Some of our passengers remained on board during the transit
stop in Bristol while the cabin crew prepared to board some
joining passengers for the next leg to Cardiff.

Back in the '90s, our cockpit doors were not locked and
there were no rules about going into lockdown on the flight
deck in the case of badly behaved or disruptive passengers.

We were busy with cockpit preparations for the next flight
when one of the cabin crew burst in and announced that if I
was not going to reprimand one of the passengers, then she was
going to take the matter into her own hands. She had taken

exception to disparaging comments from one of the transit passengers about 'the female captain'. I cannot explain why, but at the time I was in the mood to go into battle. Maybe because my cabin crew were so fiercely protective and supportive of me that I felt I owed it to all of us to stand up to this guy.

I admire how cabin crew are able to remain polite even in the face of extreme rudeness and abuse from passengers. I did not have any passenger politeness training, but as I strode from the flight deck towards seat 5A, I did consider how I would approach this guy. As luck would have it, row four was vacant so I moved in there, leant over, and folded my arms across the back of seat 4A. I could see the passenger was a short guy, about middle-forties, sitting slightly more upright and looking at me ... with a blank expression on his face. At the same time, I was aware that some other male passengers seated across the aisle appeared to know him. I recognized that all of them were English. Both of my cabin crew were frozen to their spots and were giving the situation their full attention.

"So," I said. Not "So, Sir" or anything else more polite—and with my four bars in full view. "So, I hear you seem to have a problem with female pilots." He was taken aback and could not utter anything coherent or intelligent, just a few, "Well I...well I...." I decided to help the conversation along. "So, don't you think it is about time you moved into the '90s?" As I said these words, I felt a slight nagging twinge that maybe the chief pilot might get a bad behaviour report across his desk, but it was in for a penny, in for a pound, as they say in England, so I continued.

The guys across the aisle burst into laughter and called out, "He's not even in this century." I put on my condescending smile and stared wide-eyed at 5A. He finally managed to find his voice and said, "You're Australian, aren't you?" What a fantastic observation, I thought! Then he added, "I think I have flown with you before."

Bingo! Come in spinner! Immediately I responded, "And did you get there last time?" More hilarious laughter from his travelling companions who were by now really enjoying the sideshow. 5A was no longer upright and had started to curl in towards the window. "Yes," he replied.

"Great. Then there is good chance that it might happen again," I said. I had an absolute victory here, but the nagging twinge returned, and I thought if I pushed this any further I could wind up in trouble, so I made an honourable retreat with head held high, back to the flight deck.

My two cabin crew were elated and strode through the cabin with renewed presence and pride. My co-pilot was bemused by the situation and intrigued by our English passenger's outward display of chauvinism. We had an uneventful flight to Cardiff and then back to Amsterdam. Nothing more was ever heard from 5A.

In 2016, I operated a flight on an A320 from Sydney to Coffs Harbour, along with one of our female co-pilots. As the passengers were disembarking, there was a request from a little girl to visit the flight deck. *Of course she could.* I was completely taken aback when she appeared. There she was, decked out in a homemade pilot's uniform, complete with the hat. My six-year-old passenger had her heart set on becoming an airline pilot. Her mother explained that this was all she thought about and that she wore her pilot's uniform whenever she went anywhere. What an amazing little girl she was and one who I hope one day will realize her dream.

Deborah joined Australia's Ansett Airlines in 1980. In July of 2012 Deborah went on to fly for Tiger Airways and is currently a check/training captain on the Airbus 320 based in Sydney. When not flying, her favorite thing is spending time with her husband and son.

Two Ferry Flights in the Early '70s
by Mary Bush Shipko

Flight of the Gooney Birds

We got our green light for takeoff from the Davis-Monthan Air Force Base control tower in Tucson. Eager to get going, I swung the DC-3 out onto the runway and shoved the power levers forward. My co-pilot, Charlotte, locked the tail wheel and scanned the instrument panel as we rolled down the runway. We held our breath, wondering how the old WWII plane would do. It was 1974 and the first time this particular airplane had flown in more than a decade. To our relief, everything seemed fine. We were ferrying a retired military DC-3 to Ft. Meyers, Florida, one of a fleet of ten airplanes. Of the Douglas DC-3s in our group, probably a few of them would just be used for spare parts, and that wasn't too comforting a thought right then.

We were empty, no cargo, so the tail of our stripped-down DC-3 popped up around 55 knots. Charlotte called out takeoff speed and I lifted off.

After establishing a positive rate of climb, I called, "Gear up."

Charlotte raised the gear as the desert landscape and the "boneyard" slipped away. We were on our way.

Charlotte assisted me in the rest of her duties as co-pilot, and we both said a prayer that the plane would not develop a mechanical problem of any kind. This was going to be a follow-the-leader type of flight, since only the lead plane had a radio. Charlotte and I were the only female flight crew.

"Are you sisters?" the guys had asked. Close up, we did not look alike, but from across the ramp, we were about the same height, 5'6", and of the same medium build and shape. We were the same age, 25, and we both had fair complexions and blonde hair. We were mere acquaintances—just knew of each other and little else—but we became fast friends on the trip, sisters-in-arms. We had both been freelancing, picking up jobs wherever we could.

For this job, we happened to be flying together, but most of the time we were in the same position, as first officers on the large aircraft and single pilots in the small aircraft. This trip was different; I had received my Airline Transport Pilot rating and type rating on the DC-3 on November 22, 1974, about a month before this trip, so I was qualified to fly left seat. While it was not my first trip as captain, it was one of the first few. As all new captains, I was anxious to have a good flight and naturally began to breathe a little easier as we gained altitude, putting a kind of safety net between any trouble and its resolution. We had a fairly decent glide ratio, but I quietly hoped I wouldn't have to use my brand-new glider rating on this trip. Vibrations and noises seemed normal but loud, like a factory with thirty-thousand machines all going at once.

We were on a VFR (visual flight rules), daylight-only, ferry permit. We had received a briefing before we took off; generally, we were to keep the lead plane in sight and maintain our place in the fleet. Charlotte and I were number five for takeoff. The nine of us without a radio had been given green lights from the tower for takeoff in lieu of a radio call. This is standard procedure if there is no communication between an airplane and the tower.

The "boneyard" had been impressive to see. I had heard stories of thousands of obsolete aircraft, lined up, row after row, but I wasn't sure I believed it; but it was like that back then and is still the same today. In the early '60s, DC-3s arrived there *en masse.* The military decided they were technologically obsolete, useless. The workhorse of WWII, often credited as the plane that won the war, was now cast aside like an old lover. Lee County Mosquito Control and the cargo operators of South Florida were going to breathe new life into them.

It was a great adventure for both Charlotte and me. I had never been out west. The West, wild and rugged, yet majestic with its peaks and valleys. I could not wait to see it. Most of my flying, as well as Charlotte's, had been out of the South Florida area to points south. I had been flying DC-6 cargo flights out of the northwest corner of Miami International Airport. I also flew out of Fort Lauderdale-Hollywood International. Charlotte had been flying as first officer on a DC-3 for a local regional airline based in Puerto Rico.

Charlotte and I being accepted as a female flight crew was a rite of passage. Both of our dads were pilots, but this time we weren't with our dads, sitting in the passenger seats; instead, we were the pilots. Many of the other pilots and mechanics who were part of this operation regarded us with respect and affection. Both of our dads had done a variety of flying that included crop dusting and mosquito spraying, and some of the men knew them and had worked with them.

I climbed out at 500 feet per minute, leveled off at 5000 feet, and called for the cruise checklist. We were headed to Lee County, Florida, where the local mosquito control had purchased the ten planes. Our first stop was an overnight in Baton Rouge, Louisiana.

I leaned out the fuel flow to the engines and synched them. The engines were humming, a very comforting sound. I had a friend who was a flight attendant on a DC-3 for a small charter company. She got fired because she fell asleep, and she told me that the sound of the engines put her to sleep.

The engines hummed, and we kept our companions in sight, especially the lead plane, and then we kicked back a little for a well-deserved break. Charlotte lit a cigarette. I motioned to her, and reluctantly she opened her side window. Ah, it's great to be captain, I thought. It was the first time I did not have to put up with cigarette smoke.

The weather this late fall day couldn't have been better. A few clouds dotted the horizon, and visibility was excellent, which allowed us to see forever. Light winds and high pressure ensured good weather to our destination. Our flight plan was due east from Tucson along the path of what is I-10 today. We flew over Houston's Hobby Airport and had the Gulf of Mexico off our right wing tip. We did not fly as the crow flies. It was prudent to stay over land with plenty of airports available.

As the cities and airports slipped by, we knew we were getting close to Baton Rouge. As we started letting down, after about eight hours of flight, I spotted the 450-foot Louisiana capitol building in Baton Rouge. From what I could see, things were going as planned. I let down and spaced our plane approximately five miles apart from the plane in front of us. Was this the correct airport? I wondered. Shouldn't it be bigger? Like a flight of albatross coming in to land on a beach full of bewildered sand pipers, we landed at the small grass strip airport, where I am sure no DC-3 had been since the war—if ever.

We were at the wrong airport. The airport was so small that when one DC-3 was on the runway and another on the taxiway, their wing tips could kiss, and ours did. A few minor scrapes on the aircraft wing tips was the outcome. Once repaired with duct tape and deemed airworthy by the mechanics traveling with us, we continued on.

The airport had no fuel, and all of us needed to refuel. After stretching our legs, our lead captain—a little chagrined—had us pile back in our planes for the short hop to the intended airport.

The second airport was larger, had paved runways, but no tower. With only one radio, it was necessary to avoid controlled airports. Landing without communications at a controlled airport is considered an emergency. Without a radio, communication is done through lights. Green is okay to land or takeoff. It is also cheaper to use a small local airport, as services, including fuel, are less expensive.

The next day we traded duties and Charlotte did the flying. Again the weather was perfect. We were once again the fifth to take off. Everything seemed normal, the engines, instruments, control surfaces, vibrations, noises, and smells. We over flew Pensacola and the panhandle of Florida and then took a right turn to fly down the gulf side of Florida. We flew over Tampa and Fort Myers and then descended into Lehigh West Airport, an old military field. Charlotte slid her window open as she lit her final cigarette, although I could tell she was less than happy about it. I don't think there was any heat in the aircraft. We had dressed warmly, and the temperature was tolerable. It was common for the heaters to be inoperative in these aircraft.

The guys we flew with were both humored and awed by us. I recall one conversation I overheard in Tucson.

"We have stewardesses on this flight?"

"Oh no, they're one of the flight crews. The one with the short hair is the captain."

"You're shitting me, right?"

"Nope, they're part of the crew."

"I bet they slept their way through training."

"Don't you know who they are? Why, I flew with their dads. The captain is Charlie Bush's daughter. She's typed in a C-46. The -3 must be a cakewalk for her. Hell, man, I guarantee you her old man taught her, and the same with the co-pilot. Those two could probably fly circles around us."

"Thanks," I said to the man talking, as I walked by and winked.

Arriving at our destination, Lehigh West Airport, we gathered up our personal things—cactuses and other souvenirs we had collected in Arizona—picking them out of our old gentle giant with all its quirks, smells, and oddities. The DC-3 is sometimes thought of as a "real man's" airplane, but I think of it as a woman's airplane, gentle and forgiving. The large wing area makes low speed maneuverability in the air excellent. Empty on a short final approach, you seem to almost hover.

That large wing area gave the DC-3 its nickname, Gooney Bird. It is a shared name of both the albatross and the DC-3. In the Pacific Theater arena of WWII, the DC-3/C-47 and the albatross were both common sights. They share a long wing span and large wing area. This makes slow flight and short field landings easy. Some say they look awkward or "gooney" when they take off.

Just as we started to let the cabin door down to leave, a ramp worker drove up.

"Hi," he said with a big smile, as he peered inside the plane, looking up and down the empty plane. Then he looked back at us and said, "Who's driving?"

Mary Bush was the first woman pilot for Hughes Airwest. She was hired in 1976.

Charlotte Wall was the first woman pilot for Southern Airlines. She was hired in 1977.

Douglas DC-7: Three-engine Ferry Flight from Aruba to Miami, 1973

In 1973, I was flying for Conner Airlines out of Miami International in the northwest corner, usually referred to as Corrosion Corner. This nickname was for the old WWII transport reciprocating airplanes that many of the operators used. The operators of these small freight companies were often called "fly-by-night." It sounded more exotic than it was. In reality, you took off from Miami in the middle of the night in order to be at the Caribbean and Latin America by early morning. I went to bed in the afternoon to get up at midnight. I dressed quietly, took my flight bag, and left.

For this particular flight, I arrive at the hangar just off of 36th Street and go to check-in.

"Good morning," I say to the other pilots and crews entering the crew room. It's about 1:15 a.m. The crew room is a busy place. Conner Airlines will have four departures this morning.

"Hola," Captain Che says with a big smile. Born in Cuba, he prefers Spanish even though his English is very good. He learned to fly in the Cuban Air Force. Like many Cubans, he came to the United States when Castro came to power. Cargo operators were one place he could fly.

"Good morning to you," Kyle, the flight engineer says with a smile.

I nod a good morning to other crews and settle down to our flight briefing.

"All right, let's go over our flight and weather," Captain Che says. "First, Kyle, did you complete the walk around and pre-flight?"

"Yes sir, we are all set," Kyle says.

"Good. This morning we will take off for Aruba and, after unloading, we will head to Medellin, Columbia. There we will spend the night. Once loaded, we will fly nonstop back to Miami. Our first leg to Aruba will be close to five hours. Are there any questions?" Che asks. This was a regular routing. We would be flying for Antillean Airways (ALM) going down and for Aerolineas coming back. Conner was contracted to fly their freight. Back then most of the Caribbean and Latin American airlines had a surplus of cargo and contracted with operators like Conner to fly it down.

We head out to the aircraft on the ramp. The moonlight bounces off the aluminum fuselage, giving a luster to the old DC-7CF, and a feeling of fondness warms me. I love to fly these old four-engine aircraft all over the Caribbean, and what great experience I was getting.

We climb the freight ladder and stow our things. Engines started, we taxi to 9L, the active runway. We are heavy, so our takeoff roll is long and seems slow to get to lift-off speed. After take-off, the captain picks up our heading, a gentle turn to the southeast. The early morning is still and quiet; the stars shine bright as we pass over Miami's famed beaches. The ocean shimmers with an iridescent quality. The beauty outside the cockpit must have captured all of our imaginations, for we flew along in silence for some time.

About an hour after departure, I call Miami Center and report our position. Our flight path is keeping the Bahamas off our left wing, and Cuba off our right wing tip. Hispaniola is also on our right side. Just past the Dominican Republic, the San Juan (Puerto Rico) Center handles position reports. Just past Punta Cana, on the tip of the Dominican Republic, we make a right turn and head straight to Aruba.

The sun rose at about the halfway point of the 1,130 mile trip. The flight engineer became concerned with the number four engine during the last half of the way down. Kyle, like most of the engineers, had been military trained; they were not pilots, but mechanics. He could not get the readings on his instrument panel to his liking. Kyle adjusted and readjusted the throttles the rest of the way, but did not shut it down. We were heavily loaded and we really needed the power from that engine. An engine at reduced power was still preferable to nothing.

Closer to Aruba, we were handed off to TTPP/Piarco Center. They control the Eastern Caribbean. Their coverage starts right after San Juan Center. I made our position report about an hour out.

Aruba was part of the ABC islands in the Lesser Antilles. As we approached the island, I started to make out the north coastline, wild and barren, a moonscape. The semi-arid climate supports scrubby, desert-like trees. The ever-present trade winds blow 15 to 20 knots every day. As I viewed the island from the cockpit, I noticed that everything grew at a slant on the coast.

We descended and entered a left base for Runway 11 at Queen Beatrix International Airport. After clearing customs, we went to be unloaded. While the aircraft was being unloaded, mechanics from ALM came over to help our engineer diagnose the engine problem.

They worked on it for about four hours while we were being unloaded and finally said they would have to get a ferry permit and return us to base. That meant that we had to cancel the rest of our trip. The engines on the DC-7 were the same as those on a Constellation, so I had some experience with these often-temperamental engines. The 3350s were prone to overheating and were not as reliable as the 2800s on the DC-6.

The company secured a ferry permit, and we prepared to make a three-engine takeoff. I would fly, and Kyle would increase power on the three operating engines, and the captain would be free to command us.

Due to Aruba's strategic value, the runway is exceptionally long for an island that size, 9000 feet long and 148 feet wide. The US Air Force used the island as an air base during WWII. The runway was a big help for us, as it let us use a longer than normal takeoff roll. We started out with balanced power, one engine on each side. Then the engineer brought the number one engine on line.

"V1," the captain called.

I noted the call and knew V2 was imminent. I maintained my rudder pressure, increasing slightly in coordination with the advancing throttle on the number one engine.

"V2," The captain called.

I rotated and scanned my instruments while making sure we were flying in a straight line and maintaining a positive rate of climb.

"Gear up and flaps up," I called.

We remained on the same heading, straight and level, until we gained a thousand feet.

Out of 5000 feet, everything still looked good. In fact, the takeoff had gone fine. We established cruise and made a beeline for Miami. Our hope was that we would not have another engine problem on the way back. Overheating on the three remaining engines was possible. Twelve years earlier, my dad had lost one engine flying back from Haiti in a DC-3. An hour out of Miami, he lost the other engine, due to the strain put on it by the loss of the first engine. He ditched the airplane, got out on the wing ready to evacuate, shined his flash light down and saw sand. He was in three feet of water! There was really no good place to land between Aruba and Miami, and none of the islands would have much in the way of maintenance to help.

Fortunately, the flight home turned out to be uneventful. It was strange to look out and see one propeller stationary.

The weather in Miami was 2000 to 3000 and scattered with light and variable winds.

"That wasn't too bad," I said to the flight engineer before our debriefing started. "Why, our typical flight time was extended by only seventeen minutes."

"We have a good captain," he said. "You cannot imagine the ills that can befall a three-engine takeoff. Many result in accidents. Some can't stay on the center line, but some get airborne and then can't clear obstacles. We were lucky. We had a great runway, no obstacles, and a good captain."

"But I was doing the flying," I said, "not the captain."

"Yes, and you did a good job. But the management of the flight was a captain's, and he made all the right decisions. You're too young to know the perils of what we did. The last three-engine takeoff I was part of never got airborne and ended up in the ditch. I was lucky to have lived."

"Why did you land in the ditch?" I asked.

"The captain let the aircraft get away from him. First off, we didn't have a long runway, just average. The runway that we had today was a luxury; few runways are that long and wide. I could see a problem developing. I tried to warn him that it was starting to veer to the left, but he ignored me. I'm not a pilot, right?" he said. "By the time he tried to correct, it was too late."

"Being ignored—I get that a lot too," I said.

"Yes, I guess you would," he said.

Mary was hired by Hughes Airwest in 1976 as a first officer on the Fairchild F-27. She retired as a second officer on the B727. Read more flying stories by Mary in her memoir, *AVIATRIX*.

Mary and Charlotte.

Three Flying Adventures: Danger in the Dark, The Tigers' Den, and Severe Turbulence
by Norah O'Neill

Danger in the Dark

The day started routinely in the Fairbanks, Alaska winter when I flew for Alaska Central Air in 1974; I had no premonition of peril to come. I was sipping my first cup of coffee at 6 a.m. and deciding on my fashion statement of the day, which mainly meant choosing the color of turtleneck and scarf I would put on with my long underwear, wool sweater, down vest, padded overalls, and long down parka. Sometimes I got zippy and wore rainbow-striped socks under my knee-high mukluks. No one could see them, but I knew they were there.

I started my plane's preflight at 6:30 a.m. and topped off the fuel tanks after checking the weight of the load I would carry to Tanana. It was minus 40° F, and I was careful to keep my glove liners on when I took off my elbow-length down-and-canvas mittens to unscrew the gas caps. My plane had not made it into the hangar the night before, so I put an electric heater under the instrument panel to heat the instruments to a functioning temperature. The skies were clear, but the forecast was for snow later. I didn't know when I might be flying solely by reference to gauges. I'd had midnight medivacs where the artificial horizon did not erect itself into usefulness until an hour into the flight. I didn't want to experience that problem again.

I sold tickets for my flight at the ticket counter in the Fairbanks International Airport Terminal and checked in the baggage. "Baggage" in the Alaskan bush was loosely defined. I'd had people check in such things as an unwrapped moose haunch as baggage. Sacks of groceries, brown bags of booze bottles, chemical toilets, and furniture were not uncommon check-ins. If it wasn't dangerous and we could fit it in and hope to deliver it in one piece, we took it. The passengers watched me load the last of the bags as they shuffled out onto the icy ramp. After they strapped in, I hopped into the pilot's seat of the Cherokee Six.

Only one of the six wanted to get out when he saw who his pilot was. That was a good day for me. I explained that I was doing the Tanana run that week, and if he wanted a male pilot, he would have to wait until next week. He decided to stay but complained loudly to the other passengers: "What's the world coming to? Someone should be keeping her in the kitchen where she belongs."

"Sir, if you continue talking so loudly, I am going to be distracted from my work. You want me to be able to concentrate, don't you?" I smiled at him over my shoulder. He shut up.

That load of people got off in Tanana and more boarded to go further down the Yukon to the village at Ruby and the Air Force Base at Galena. Five hours later, I headed my plane down the snowy runway at Galena and headed home with six adults and one child on board. It was dark then, and the forecasted snow had started. Despite having headwinds, I expected to be home in less than three hours.

I settled in and dimmed the cabin lights. Only one passenger kept her reading light illuminated. It was a cozy flight, the steady hum of the engine lulling people to sleep. I wasn't using my radio because I was out of Center's range for that part of the flight. I planned to check back in with them when I was halfway between Tanana and Fairbanks, somewhere over the Minto Lake region.

The first anomaly my scanning of the instruments picked up was my ammeter gauge showing a discharge. That was unusual. The alternator belt, rotating behind the propeller, ran the alternator and usually provided all the juice I needed, as well as keeping the battery charged. But gauges were notoriously unreliable in Alaskan winters (I hoped), and there was nothing I could do about a problem with the alternator while in flight. I needed to land as soon as possible, but there was nowhere to set down before Fairbanks.

As a precautionary measure, I turned off the cabin lights and got out my two-celled flashlight. I tried my radio. Reception was faint and getting fainter. I broadcast into the blind that I was having electrical problems and would probably arrive in Fairbanks without a radio. I confirmed my estimated time of arrival and hoped that someone in the air would transmit it to Fairbanks. I was going to be arriving incommunicado during a snowstorm, and there were other planes out there; the skies were busy during the building of the Alaskan Pipeline.

I turned off my rotating beacon and left my small green and red navigation lights on. I turned off the navigation and communication radios, hoping that I would be able to preserve some charge to use in shooting an instrument approach to Fairbanks. With that thought, I also turned off my navigation lights.

· What instruments would be left to help me find the airport? The magnetic compass was fairly useless, but I could at least bracket a heading with it. *Good old needle-ball turn indicator ought to be okay, or was it electric?* I reviewed which gauges were electric and which ran off the pitot static system. That air-pressurized system should be all right, but I had forgotten the ever-present snow. The heating for the pitot head, placed on the side of the plane's nose, was electric. If the tiny air-intake hole iced over, I'd lose my airspeed indicator. If the static hole iced, I would lose my altimeter. It was as if thinking made that so—I looked up to see my airspeed rising to the redline of overspeed and then peg out at the top of the gauge. My altimeter started to fall. I switched my altimeter source to alternate air. It rose again sluggishly. *I'm going to lose all my instruments. How can I get these people down safely? Stop. Don't think about that. Think about what you do have. Make a plan.*

I was less than an hour out, and I knew my heading was going to get me near Fairbanks. I also knew the time of my last position point and how many minutes would have to tick by before I was over Fairbanks.

The biggest problem was going to be the descent. Too early, and I would hit the hills. Too late, and I would hit the mountains. With no reliable altimeter and no visibility, I had no assurance that I wouldn't just fly into the ground before I broke out. I'd lost the readouts from my fuel-quantity gauges, but my fuel-pressure gauges still worked, so I knew I had fuel. I still had the oil pressure readout. My directional gyro and my artificial horizon operated off a vacuum pump, so they'd be with me until the end.

I was flying now with a flashlight illuminating my gauges. *What if I need both hands? How long could I hold this cold metal tube in my teeth?* I tested that out. The kid in the seat next to mine made no comment about my sucking on my flashlight. I looked at him watching me and grinned around the metal in my mouth.

Someone in back asked what had happened to her reading light. "Precautionary shutdown," I advised. I didn't know how much to tell my passengers, if anything. I didn't want to panic them. What could they do to help? Did they have the right to know we might not make it down safely? I did enlist the aid of the boy in the copilot's seat, just in case. I showed him where to shine the flashlight on the instruments that were most important to me. We made a game of it. I handed him my watch, and he practiced calling out ten-second intervals to me. We laughed.

My passengers were beginning to ask questions, and I was afraid my voice would betray my tension, but I was surprised that I sounded so calm, so bored really. Where did that cool come from?

My calculated descent point arrived. We should be east of Nenana over flat lake-filled terrain, hopefully near the meandering curves of the Tanana River. I hoped to descend to near the river's surface and follow it east to Fairbanks. If I could find it and stay over it, I could get home without hitting anything.

My eleven-year-old copilot started the timer as I eased the throttles back to the place I knew, from hundreds of hours in this type of plane, to be the spot on the throttle pedestal that I usually set the power at for descent. It was rather like driving a familiar car and knowing that just so much foot pressure would give me thirty miles an hour on the flat.

Power set, nose of the plane pushed over to just a hair under the artificial horizon, I trusted that we were sinking at 500 feet per minute at cruise speed. In two minutes, we were a thousand feet lower. I could not see forward or below. Two more minutes and another thousand feet down. I still couldn't see anything, and I couldn't get any further forward in my seat without unbuckling my seat belt. After another minute of sinking into what was beginning to feel like an abyss, I caught a change in the darkness below. I could see white and black areas, like a pinto's back. The white areas unblurred and became rounded, snow-covered frozen lakes. A snow snake curved at their edges—the river.

I continued my descent and flew into cottony white. Everything above, below, and in front of me was again obscured in cloud. I didn't know I was holding my breath until we broke out of the clouds again and I heard it panting out. *I can't lose sight of the ground again. I can't descend lower and still hope to break out in time.* I pointed the plane's nose up the river and added power.

I flew through thickening snow flurries but kept the ground in sight. A passenger commented on the close-up view of the river below and the hills rising blackly above our left wing. "Why don't we make this approach more often? It's more fun than higher up." *Why indeed.* The night-lights of Fairbanks glowed through the white in the distance.

Now came another tricky part. Hopefully, an alert air traffic controller had noticed the tiny blip of 5TA disappear from his radar screen just before he was scheduled to hear from it. Hopefully, someone had noticed the return echo of a plane winding its way up the river to the city. Hopefully, he saw the blip approaching and was clearing the runway for it to land.

I saw the lights of Fairbanks International Airport emerge from around a bend in the river. I lined up with the main runway and slowed and did the prelanding checklist while I stared out toward the runway ahead, looking for other planes. I was clinching my controls, prepared to turn sharply to avoid a collision.

I landed. The tower gave me light signals for a taxi clearance, and I motored on to park next to the terminal.

The enormity of my physical reaction to an hour of adrenaline rush and fear held in check did not become apparent until I opened the pilot's door to hop out onto the wing and jump to the ground to offload baggage. I swung my legs over the wing, pushed my feet to its surface, grabbed the top of the door for leverage, and tried to stand up. I could not. My knees folded down and I plunked into a pile. The phrase "my knees gave out" took on a new aspect. *Wow. Now I know what that means.*

My passengers got out by themselves. They waited, stomping in the cold and snow by the baggage compartment door and eyeing me sitting on the wing, until one of them opened the door himself and heaved the cases onto the ramp.

"Nice flight," one called, turning to the terminal.

"Yeah, thanks," said another.

"I had fun. Thanks for letting me help fly," said my pint-sized copilot.

"Anytime," I called, waving them on. Alone on the wing in the dark, I scooched to the edge, swung my legs downward and clung to the side of the plane as I lowered my weight. I stood, walked back, and shut the baggage compartment door. Then, I climbed back in for the taxi to the hangar. I fueled the plane and put it to bed for the night, leaving a note for the mechanics. I could see that my alternator belt was gone.

"Hey, Norah, howzit goin'?" asked the arriving night janitor.

"Just fine. Long day though," I replied and walked to my car.

Pilots don't cry or talk about being scared. I put my shoulders back.

I was a pilot.

The Tigers' Den, 1976

I was only going to get one chance. I *had* to convince four men that I could do something no woman had been allowed to do before.

"Hey, are you the girl pilot?"

"Yes, I'm down from Alaska to see about a pilot's job with Flying Tigers."

"Oh, great. We girls have been waiting for you," said the chief pilot's secretary. "Tigers has never interviewed a girl pilot before. Lots of the men don't want you here." She laughed. "Time for them to get out of the dark ages. I hope they hire you."

Big smile. "Thanks. I'm so nervous I can't walk straight. And these heels." I rolled my eyes, and we looked down at my serviceable, chunky-heeled brown shoes. *God, don't let me fall flat on my face.*

"I'll walk you to the door," she offered and squeezed my hand.

"Hey guys, she's here!" She introduced me and gave me a gentle shove through the office door.

Four suit-clad men rose from behind an imposing desk and introduced themselves as Flying Tiger Captains Oakley Smith, Dick Stratford, Al Grant, and Dick Keefer. I was glad for my dad's early lessons in the proper way to shake hands. Step forward while extending your hand, always maintaining eye contact; squeeze firmly; break the hold crisply. Three of my interviewers had obviously gotten the same hand-shaking lesson, but the fourth turned our hand clasp into a bone-crushing, macho contest of he who cries out in pain first loses. Luckily, I have a high pain threshold, and our contest appeared to be a draw.

They invited me to be seated. I sank into the too-soft couch, grateful that I was no longer taller than two of the men. (I knew some men had problems with my towering over them, and my heels had raised me to over six feet.) I had wrapped my waist-length bright red hair into a conservative businesslike bun.

I didn't have a role model, had never even met another woman pilot. I didn't know what kind of questions I would be asked, but assumed there would be many technical aviation questions—about engines and aerodynamics, Federal Aviation Administration rules and regulations, licensing, and instrument flying. I was certain they would ask about my hours of flight experience. Because I had acquired many hours in very few years in the Alaskan bush, I thought that my flight time might look like "Parker pen" time to them.

Oakley Smith, Vice President of Flight Operations, carefully explained to me that laws had been passed making it illegal to ask a woman any questions in an interview that were not asked of male applicants. He supposed that I, of course, was aware of this.

I had been in the Alaskan bush for a long time, totally immersed in flying, and living, almost literally, in airplanes. I was quietly playing my own part in the Women's Liberation Movement, but I was woefully ignorant of current events.

"That's interesting," I said. "I wasn't aware of that law. But, surely, if you've never interviewed a woman pilot before, there must be some questions you would like to ask about how I might work in an all-male workplace. You have my permission to ask me anything you want." In my youthful naiveté, I had not a clue to the doors I had just given them leave to open.

"Well, thank you for your understanding," one of the panel said to me with a smile. "Tell me about your periods."

Swallow. Blink. "My periods? What about them?"

"How are your periods?" he elucidated. "How do they affect your reliability at work? How do they affect your flying? I noticed that you took four days of sick leave in the last three years. Were those sick days because of your periods?"

I was definitely *not* following the questioner's logic. My brain raced with the implied math of how many days in my period I had had in the previous three years, at 7 days a month times 12 times 3. Surely if I had had problem periods, I would have missed more than four days of work.

"I have *never* missed work because of my period."

He couldn't let the subject go. I surmised that he was married to someone who must have to take to her bed for days at a time. I had heard of such women and sympathized with them, but I was not one of them.

"Can you honestly say that your periods have *never* affected your flying?" he pressed on.

I thought of an incident in Alaska a few months back, flying an empty airplane home to Fairbanks after a very long day on a cross-state cargo charter. I was tired and was mildly troubled by menstrual cramps. At the same time, another of Alaska Central Air's pilots was also returning home in an empty plane after a long day of back-to-back medical evacuations on the Alaskan Pipeline. He fell asleep in the cockpit and overflew Fairbanks, his plane heading toward the mountains beyond. What saved his life was one of his engines quitting because of fuel starvation. The subsequent swerving of his plane awakened him just before he would have flown into the side of a mountain.

I thought of that night in Alaska and looked my nagging questioner in the eye. "Oh, yes, my period *has* affected my flying. My cramps have kept me awake on long, boring freight runs."

They asked about my plans for marriage and children. I thought I would do that someday, yes. They wondered if I would quit then to stay home and raise my children.

"Wow," I responded, "have a lot of your pilots done that? I mean, produced a child, then left it up to someone else to feed him and send him to college? It doesn't sound very responsible, and I like to think that I shoulder my obligations better than that."

They asked whether I liked to party. In the Alaskan bush, on call twenty-four hours a day, there wasn't much time for going to parties. I told the interviewers that I liked to party but no longer drank alcohol, so I didn't think going to parties would interfere with my flying.

Oakley Smith wanted to know what I was going to do when someone made a pass at me in the cockpit.

"In the cockpit? Surely there isn't time for that?" I exclaimed.

"It *will* happen," Captain Smith said firmly. "What are you going to do?"

The men all laughed and sat up straighter awaiting my answer. In Alaska, if I were on a two-pilot crew, we usually had passengers on board and our cockpit was open to their perusal. We tried to present a professional presence. I was especially conscious of passenger eyes on me because so many of them had expressed open horror that a female was in charge of the plane. One of the main reasons I had applied to Flying Tigers was that they were the world's largest cargo airline, and I never wanted to fly passengers again. I had illusions about what flying for a "real" airline meant. I thought it meant total professionalism and saying goodbye to many of the problems I had had because I was a "girl" pilot. My education in that area was just leaving grade school and getting ready for junior high.

These men were waiting for an answer to a question I had not dreamed of being asked.

This was not a pilot question but a woman question. I answered as a woman.

"I would handle a pass in the cockpit the same way I would handle one on the ground."

"So what do you do on the ground?" a man asked.

"I say either 'yes, please' or 'no, thank you'."

The men laughed and exchanged glances.

Next, they explored how I had racked up so many flight hours in so short a time. With relief, I produced my logbooks and paystubs. A job-seeking pilot might fabricate flight hours, but no employer would have paid him for them. I think they were relieved to know that I really had flown as much as I said I had.

Dick Stratford said, "Someone with thousands of hours in the Alaskan bush has to be either very, very good or very, very lucky. I hope you're both."

We then swapped stories about flying in Alaska, which several of them had done. This led to the only fun I had in the interview. I got to listen to them "hangar fly," a pilot pastime of sitting safely on the ground and telling stories about how a pilot cheated death by bringing an airplane home against insurmountable odds. I have yet to meet a pilot who can resist hangar flying at any given opportunity.

I listened in fascination as one of them told a story about a Tiger crew flying a World War II vintage C-46 on the northern slope of Alaska during a white out. A "white out" describes visibility commonly encountered during a snowstorm when the horizon disappears into unending white above and below it. In that region of very few and very primitive navigational aids, a whiteout has been deadly for many pilots. Some of the most prominent landmarks on aviation maps for the area are wrecks of old planes.

The Tigers miraculously found the airstrip they were searching for but lost sight of it during their descent and motored on blindly. Noticing that their airspeed was decreasing, they added power. Their airspeed did not increase but went to zero. It took long moments for them to realize what had happened. They had flown their airplane into the ground. The billowing cushion of snow had prevented them from feeling the ground contact, and their view from the cockpit window had not changed one iota—it was still zero. They had made a good landing if one went by the common pilot's definition—any one you can walk away from is a good landing.

I had flown C-46's out of Fairbanks and was in awe of anyone who could fly them well.

They were the most difficult planes to land and park that I had ever been in. While those Tiger pilots talked about captaining the C-46, I wanted more than anything to be able to fly with them one day and to hear more of their stories. For me, they were history come alive.

As their hanger flying abated, one of the men noted that I had C-46 time and asked me how much fuel a C-46 held. I realized, in a panic, that I did not know. Here I was finally being asked a technical question and I *did not know* the answer. My brief dreams of becoming an airline pilot were flying out the window. I explained, with sinking hope, that the C-46's I had flown were oil tankers and were flown visual flight rules only during the summer in order to replenish heating-fuel storage tanks of remote villages. We were always at maximum gross weight and fueled the plane with just enough gas to get to the destination. I had never seen the C-46 full of gas.

"I don't know how many gallons of fuel the C-46 holds," I said squaring my shoulders. I was going to take the flunking of this interview like I imagined a man would. I forced a smile and asked the panel of my judges what the correct answer was.

"Captain Smith, you captained the C-46. How much fuel did it hold?"

"Damned if I can remember," he replied. "Do any of you know?"

They did not. I was amazed. How could these gods of Tiger aviation not know the answer to a question they had asked?

The time allotted for my interview was up. They stood to see me out. I didn't have any idea what impression I had made on them. I didn't know that it was not cool to ask, so I did ask.

"Do I have the job?"

They had surprised looks on their faces. "We'll call you if you get the job," they promised.

My mom had flown from San Diego to be with me for the interview process in Los Angeles. We spent two more days together, while I underwent rigorous physical examinations and testing. There were other young pilots at the medical facility who had also had interviews. It seemed hopeful to us that Tigers was paying to have us examined.

I assumed we were all undergoing the same tests until an embarrassed doctor said, "Uhmm. We're not sure what to do here. We have never examined a female pilot before, and there are no spaces on the examination sheet for reporting your, umm, gynecological condition. I should, I guess, do a breast exam. Or, do you, by chance, do your own? Um," he went on, "and I guess I should do a pelvic exam, or do you have regular pap smears done? We could perhaps have your gynecologist send his latest report?"

Poor man. "I'll arrange to have my gynecologist send the paperwork to you."

I returned to work in Alaska and began waiting. Summer was our busiest flying season in Fairbanks, and I was able to forget the waiting while I flew almost around the clock.

Severe Turbulence, 1981

On a cold spring night, Captain Tom Frederickson perused the weather data for our flight from New York to Chicago and Anchorage. After noting that the current weather and forecasts for both cities were lousy, he said, "O'Neill, how good a pilot are you? I've heard some bad stories about you, but surely they can't all be true. I'm a weak pilot. I need a good copilot. Do you have much time in the 747?"

Oh, spare me. And I have to spend a week with this guy? "I'm relatively new on the plane, sir, but I'm certainly a competent pilot."

"Good," he replied. "You're flying both legs tonight. The weather is beneath my standards. I fly only when it's VFR."

What? I puzzled this over. Was he truly a low-speed pilot who always delegated the tougher flying to his copilot? Or was this a test to see if I was arrogant enough to think I could do better than my captain? Or was he trying to bolster my self-confidence by letting me know that he was relying on my doing a good job? Was I really going to fly both legs?

Chicago weather was as bad as was forecast, and I flew the leg. After landing, Tom remarked, "Good job. We'll do okay together."

We continued onward to Anchorage, where the visibility was acceptable but severe turbulence was forecast. Not too much about weather alarmed me anymore except for windshear and turbulence. It was difficult to avoid something you couldn't see. Professional pilots were expected to avoid areas that displayed the earmarks of severe weather, yet they were also expected to get the plane there on schedule. Even though no sane pilot would knowingly enter severe turbulence, we were supposed to launch the plane on time and hope that the skies would get better during the six hours it would take for us to reach our destination.

As we descended into Anchorage, the turbulence came as forecast and worsened as we lost altitude. It was the worst I had ever experienced. I struggled to keep the plane upright. Straight and level was impossible. Striving for it was taking full control inputs in every direction. I was not happy with the choreography of this ballet and asked Tom if we should start considering our alternate airport. He pointed out that other planes were still taking off and landing successfully. It's hard to explain to a company why you spent thousands of extra dollars in time and fuel going to an unscheduled airport, when other pilots were doing what you were too chicken to do. Shoulders back. Breathe deep. Motor on.

On our downwind leg, we saw a Tiger 747 take off below us. When that plane was stabilized in climb, its captain radioed all aircraft in the vicinity. "Warning. Tiger encountered 20 knots of windshear immediately after takeoff. We almost lost the plane. Watch your asses."

Tom, recognizing the voice of JD Johnson, radioed, "Hey, JD, give us the details. We're next to land."

"It's a bitch down low. Who you got flying tonight, Tom?"

"Norah's at the wheel."

"Oh, Christ, you can't let her fly it!"

"Why not? She flies better than I do."

"Because she's a woman! Everyone knows women have lousy depth perception. There's no room for any handicaps tonight."

"Lousy depth perception?"

"Yeah. All her life she's been told that six inches is actually nine inches. Can't expect her to be able to read scale on maps or judge height with accuracy."

That's one of the things I loved about Tiger pilots. When the going got rough, they started joking. It relieved the tension. I hooted at JD's new take on an old joke and the precision of his timing.

We bounced down final like an autumn leaf falling. Wing up. Wing down. Nose over. Nose up. To hell with airspeed; I could no longer ascertain which numbers the swinging needle was bracketing and couldn't believe that Tom was letting his copilot do this. He was either very stupid or very crafty. Either way, he had balls of steel. We made the runway unscathed.

On the way to the hotel, I hung limply in my seat while Tom talked layover plans. I was meeting a girlfriend and wasn't going to be with the rest of the crew.

"What are you and Lisa going to do?"

"Drink champagne and troll for hard bodies."

"Hard bodies?" Tom mulled over the word. He had never heard it before. "What do you mean, hard bodies?"

"You know, young studs with big arms and washboard stomachs," I explained. "Bodies with no flab. Young. Energetic."

He thought about that. "I guess I'm not one. What would you girls call me, soft body?"

"I think I'll stick with Captain Tom."

Lisa and I talked that night about the frightening turbulence and the macho-right-stuff coping mechanism of joking when death was imminent. Part of me was appalled that I would laugh at a penis-length quip during what might be my last moment on earth, but part of me accepted that that is how we pilots did it. To fully experience our feelings at those moments would probably have incapacitated us.

Norah was hired in 1976 by Flying Tigers as a flight engineer on the Douglas DC-8. She retired with Flying Tigers flying the Boeing 747. Norah passed away in 2017 at her home in Seattle, Washington, after a brave battle with cancer. She is survived by her two adult children, Cameron and Bren.

Norah wearing the dress motif she designed and silkscreened.

Light Air, Pink Sky [excerpted]
by Tracy Lamb

The 24th of October, 1994

The early morning air was already heavy, humid, and silent. I found myself airborne, flying out of control with only one way down. From that moment, my life as I had known it would be changed forever.

My experience with flying had been what most ordinary people encounter—an economy seat on an airliner, usually over the wing—segregated to a small personal space counting the seconds until the terrible ordeal was over.

I flew often for my work as a gemologist and jewelry designer and dreaded the thought of getting on an aircraft. I was a passenger afraid of flying.

As I lay in agony amidst the crumpled mess of my car that had just plummeted and rolled off the cliff 200 meters above, I felt like I had just been in an aircraft crash.

My spine was broken...crushed. I was unable to move. My left ankle had shattered, my neck was badly burned and bruised from the seatbelt, I was in shock from being belted with the exploding airbag. I was alone in severe pain, and strangely, the air returned again to being heavy, humid, and silent.

This was the best day of my life, and the first day of the rest of my new life.

The first of two surgeries on my spine was the most dangerous. It was also the most frightening for me. The best specialists in Australia studied my injury, while for over a week I was physically restrained on a hospital bed, not allowed to move...too frightened to move.

Several surgeons had stopped by my room at the Holy Spirit Hospital in Brisbane to meet me. Most of them had not seen this type of injury where the spinal cord had escaped unharmed after such extensive damage. All were professional, kind, and serious. I was terrified, alone, and desperately helpless.

The most difficult part of the surgery would be picking out the fragments of the shattered vertebrae from the spinal column, precariously touching my spinal cord. The surgeon gave the surgery being a success a 30% chance of success.

My eyes slowly opened to a grey mist. I could hear foggy voices and distant sounds. My mouth was dry. I croaked, "Are my toes moving, are my toes moving?"

"Yes they are, Tracy," replied someone in the intensive care unit.

Exhausted I returned to the grey mist. I had been granted my 30% chance.

If you spend six months confined to a wheelchair it changes your perspective on life, people, and relationships.

Seven months after the car accident, the metal scaffolding of titanium screws and rods were taken from my spine. I was still in a wheelchair most of the time and I had started short bursts of walking with the aid of two calipers (leg braces). I was very awkward, but I was walking!

I arrived home from the hospital the day Christopher Reeve fell from his horse in an equestrian competition, breaking his neck and becoming a quadriplegic. Stunned by this, I was reminded how lucky I was.

My son was just over two years old. What a joyous gift he was—such a handsome little bundle, even though I felt he never slept. We have a unique bond, an affection and connection that has lasted to this day. I believe my helplessness and devotion to him equally imprinted on both of us both during my recovery. I was always with him, crawling on the floor, playing on the carpet, or having him in my lap in the wheelchair.

I have a photo of us on his first birthday, a month after the accident. I was just out of the hospital. He was adorable and blissfully unaware of the plastic molded back brace holding my spine straight, assisting my non-existent muscles. He was unaware of the trauma I had suffered before being strong enough to sit and help him blow out his candles, or of the pain that activity inflicted. Being there for his first birthday is one of my most treasured memories.

As the months went by, I began to regain my strength. I started to ice skate after many years of working and being a devoted wife and new mother. In my teens skating was my passion. Now, although I limped on the ground, I glided on the ice, at least on my good ankle. Memories of grace and beauty returned. I found myself overwhelmed with gratitude and wept silently in the middle of the rink.

My marriage and my business did not survive the car accident. Both died with my old self at the base of that muddy cliff with the crumpled mess of the car. Our business had folded due to my neglect during recovery, and my husband's distractions included his departure overseas to live. I did not go bankrupt easily and this would torment my moral fiber for years to come.

I had become a single mother. I worked three jobs and needed welfare assistance to survive. Because of this I lost my home—the home in which I had hoped to raise my son, have Christmases with my grandchildren, and grow old with my husband. My car was towed away on a truck as my son and I watched. All gone. Slight bewilderment came over me at my predicament. My marriage and the dreams of the happy family we would have... all shattered. I was the child who just realized she foolishly placed all of her dreams in a fantasy akin to that of Santa Claus.

I constantly suffered ankle and back pain. I felt "used up." I was physically scarred, divorced, bankrupt, and feeling unattractive all at the tender age of twenty-six. Why was I so deflated with thoughts of, "Is this all there is for me?"

I cannot take credit for the recovery of the soul.

A friend of mine offered to cheer me up. My cheerful demeanor which had been observed by friends over the years had diminished since the accident and the breakup of our marriage. The plan was to take me on a "joy flight" in a Cessna 172. (This is a single engine plane that seats four people, four *skinny* people!)

I had never seen a small plane before. Clearly this friend did not know I had a rampant fear of flying.

"Is this it?" I gasped in horror. "It's only got one engine! I might as well sit on a whipper snipper or a lawnmower!"

Before the accident, I would have flatly refused to expose myself to the terror of getting into a small claustrophobia inducing cell and flying through the air, especially considering that I am also terrified of heights.

Now I sat in the front seat next to the pilot.

As the ground melted away, I caught my breath, but then I exhaled in silent amazement. I looked at the instrumentation and how it accurately reflected the changes in our altitude, speed, and direction.

This is a great comfort to the person who likes to measure things. Being a gemologist, I relax in predictable boundaries of science, physics, and chemistry. I had never entertained thinking about flying that way because I was afraid of it.

The pilot let me have the controls, and I felt that I became part of this metal bird, I felt free, a deep freedom as if my sprit let go and relaxed. I looked down on the houses, hundreds of them, a sea of them!

Now that I could measure the parameters of flight, the unknown, I felt that I had conquered what used to scare me. The exhilaration of this was life-changing. I wondered how may single mothers were down there, just like me, afraid of things that they could conquer. I did not feel alone in the world again.

We landed that day as the sun was setting. The air was light and pink. I had experienced such a profound connection with myself and with the greater world, I wanted more. My lungs drank in the pink twilight air. My life was a gift that I almost didn't get to experience fully. I didn't want to waste it, not for a moment.

The next day was beautiful. The weather was typical of an early summer morning, crisp warm, and happy. I hugged and kissed my son as I dropped him off at his Kindy group. Then, as if drawn to it by a giant magnet, I went to a flying school at Coolangatta Airport and asked for my first flying lesson.

I did not know how I was going to pay for this; I had no money. I could barely get by on what little I had from valuing jewelry for stores, working part-time in a friend's jewelry shop, and organizing children's birthday parties. I had no financial assistance for my son from my ex-husband who was now living Europe.

Something in my heart told me to keep believing, to focus on my dream to fly, that the universe would provide the solutions and the way. I did not really know how this was going to happen. I just did it one step at a time, just like when I learned how to walk and skate again.

Six months later, I had earned my private pilot license. I had sold my engagement ring to pay for the lessons while still working my three jobs and studying at night while my son slept. I would close my eyes at night, and the ceiling fan would turn into an aircraft propeller. I dreamt of flying.

That was over twenty-three years ago. I never looked back. I earned my commercial pilot license in 2001 and shortly after that became a flight instructor. I started a university degree in aviation and devoted myself to learning how to be the best pilot I could be.

The best flying I have done has been teaching others how to fly, seeing the look on their faces, and feeling their pride and amazement at what they can achieve. I recognize that incredible moment when one feels the same profound connection with themselves that I had felt. I think it must be realizing they are doing something they have just discovered will become their passion.

I loved to send people on their very first solo and see them park the aircraft with satisfaction and pride. I loved to relive that feeling of freedom and achievement in each of my students, from their first solo to earning their airline transport license and getting their first job.

After a life-threatening car accident, Tracy learned to fly. Her aviation career has taken her all over the world, from flying Australia's outback to managing drone teams in the Netherlands. Tracy collects vintage hats and loves eating Mexican food with her friends.

Miracle on the Hudson: US Airways Flight 1549—From Investigation to *Sully* Movie
by Lori Cline

O n January 15, 2009, I was sitting at my kitchen table working on a project when a news bulletin broke into regular television programming. A US Airways airplane had crash-landed into the icy Hudson River.

I had previously served for five years in the US Airways Flight Safety Department, including time as the director, where I maintained the safety oversight of our carrier's 2,400 takeoffs and landings a day. This position required extensive training in risk management, emergency response, and accident investigation. Combine that background with the role I was currently serving as that of a Check Airman and FAA designee in our Airbus Flight Training Department, it should have come as no surprise when my phone rang within fifteen minutes of Flight 1549 going down. My fleet captain was on the line saying,

"We're holding an airplane for you in GSO that's leaving for LGA in ten minutes. Can you fly to New York and represent the company in the NTSB's investigation of Flight 1549?" Now who says "no" to such a request? I threw some clothes into a suitcase, not knowing how long I would be gone, and went straight to the airport. There I was met by the station manager who whisked me past TSA's security to board the flight to LaGuardia where I would join the rest of the "go team" who were in the process of converging and assembling to organize for the investigation.

What we learned in the course of the weeks that followed was confirmation of the devastating effects bird strikes have on a flight, and that a "perfect storm" scenario exists due to four main factors which have created a serious bird infestation problem in our country. These include: 1) The banning of DDT in the seventies, 2) Aggressive EPA regulations that eradicated industrial waste and other contaminants from being dumped in our waterways, cleaning shorelines and ultimately creating a safe, inviting oasis for waterfowl everywhere, 3) Deforestation has impacted the smaller bird population, leaving only larger predators to dominate and, 4) The Protected Species and Migratory Bird Protection Act prevents these larger predatory birds from being hunted—period.

Ideal conditions further contribute to the problem, as 85% of all airports in our country lie within a five-mile radius to water where these birds frolic, completely protected, in the vast wide-open spaces the airport provides. Add the global warming element which precludes most birds from the need to migrate further south for winter, and what we have today is a thriving waterfowl population communing in the exact same space as the arrival and departure corridors of most of our country's biggest airports. As a result, statistics show bird strikes quadrupled in the US from 1990 to 2008. The resident

Canada goose population increased from one million in 1990 to four million in 2008. So it seems in many ways, Flight 1549's fate was an accident waiting to happen.

This issue has been squarely in the sights of airport managers across our country, and they have employed a variety of unique mitigation strategies as effective deterrents. These include twenty-four-hour bird patrols, employing everything from shepherd dogs to chase them, falcons to scare them, and sonar to confuse them; yet they continue to pose a threat. More reassuring is the lengths to which engine manufacturers have gone in the event birds ARE ingested into an operating engine. For a medium-sized bird, certification standards today require engines to withstand ingesting seven (one-and-one-half-pound) birds and still be able to sustain 75% of available thrust for five minutes following the ingestion. For large birds, they are certified to withstand one (four-pound) bird without having the engine catch fire or release dangerous shards or fragments through the engine casing. That's REALLY good news if you happen to be seated in the cabin immediately next to the engines!

Once our NTSB team confirmed that it was indeed a flock of birds that caused the aircraft's engines to seize (two eight-pound birds in each engine to be exact), our investigation centered on what procedures were provided by the manufacturer, Airbus, and what kind of training pilots receive from their operator, US Airways, to prepare a flight crew for such an encounter. Once we ensured that the crew acted in complete accordance with written standard operating procedures, we focused our attention on the burning question: *Could they have made it to a runway or was the risky water landing their only option*? This is where the *Sully* script writers went "Hollywood," suggesting that our efforts to answer this question were purposely designed to discredit Sully, the hero, when in fact, since this type accident had never happened before (it was, after all, the first successful water ditching of a major airliner in aviation history), we as the NTSB simply wanted to learn everything we could and find out whether it would have been possible to make a more conventional landing.

For this, our team of six launched to Toulouse, France, where Airbus Industries resides, to utilize their engineering simulator for our testing. There, for the better part of a week, we put ourselves through the same scenario, taking off, hitting the birds, and adding the human factors element experts believed to be a realistic timeframe to compensate for the startle factor the pilots would have experienced before addressing their emergency (35 seconds) before turning back to try and land. We focused our attempts on runways 22, 4, and 13. Airbus pilots demonstrated a landing at Teterboro, the airport eighteen miles west in New Jersey that Sully had asked about as the aircraft was rapidly descending, but the pilots were only successful in a landing there after seventeen consecutive tries. Some landings we made were successful; some were not. Often times if we made it to a runway unscathed and intact, we couldn't necessarily duplicate it again after a subsequent run. Thus, in the end we concluded that given the 208 seconds Sully had to factor his options, calculating the risk based on how fast they were falling from the sky, and gambling the potential for catastrophic consequences, the expansive watery runway lying immediately beneath him was indeed the safest choice and the only one that would ensure the safety of his aircraft, his passengers, and his crew.

And this is exactly what Director Clint Eastwood had us do in the filming of the movie based on Captain Chesley Sullenberger's book, *Highest Duty*. The initial request from Warner Brothers was to bring actors to the training center to film the simulator flying scripted for the NTSB hearing scenes, until our airline management explained that only our professional pilots could fly our simulators. They argued that since the studio only planned to do their filming in one day, it would certainly take far too long to train actors to make the scenes look realistic. Why not choose check airmen from our Standards cadre to do the work, *those of us who are most accustomed to demonstrating standard flying in a simulator environment, on command, day in and day out.* This is how I, coincidentally, became one of pilots selected to be part of the movie. It wasn't until I was seated next to him after the first landing we filmed that Mr. Eastwood learned I had actually been *THE* company representative for the NTSB's investigation. Once he became aware of this, he was most intent on questioning me to ensure the filming they were doing was precisely how we had done things during our flight testing in Toulouse. Oddly, this made me the only pilot in the movie technically playing myself—a female check airman on loan to the NTSB as a subject matter expert working as part of the team dedicated to learning everything we could about the accident. In another quirky twist, as part of our wardrobe, the six US Airways pilots chosen were given NTSB ID badges to wear for the filming, a prop you can't see in the movie scenes, but nevertheless, I had to chuckle at the name I noticed they affixed to mine which read Lydia Cantor. While they may have changed my name, the initials "LC" for Lori Cline, ceremoniously remained intact. No doubt just another uncanny coincidence!

So what's it like to spend the day with Hollywood legend, eighty-six-year-old Clint Eastwood? I found him to be the consummate professional: quiet, stoic, revered on the set, and extremely low maintenance. He shared with my copilot and I that one of the things that drew him to the story was that back in his Army days he was hitching a ride in a single seat bomber that ditched off the coast of San Francisco, so he knew what that experience was like. We filmed for seven and a half hours, and he stood almost the entire time in the cramped simulator bursting with a lot more bodies shoulder to shoulder than it normally holds. In all, he barely took more than a five-minute bathroom break the entire day. I had anticipated he would give a lot more direction than he did. Instead, he sat humbly by, watching as each of us took the simulator through the reenactment scenarios they had scripted. We were told the all-day shoot might render one and a half to two minutes on the big screen, and while we guessed much of what we filmed would end up on the cutting room floor, I was encouraged my scenes might survive when I was asked to travel to a sound stage in Atlanta to do some voiceovers. Then, folks from Warner Brothers called to ask how I wanted my name to appear in the credits, so I guessed that at least some of what I filmed had made it to the movie.

Fast forward to one year later when finally the movie was ready to be released. We were all invited to the *Sully* movie premiere, complete with red carpet paparazzi at the Lincoln Center in New York, which was the icing on the cake really. I'm not sure which "pinch myself" moment was more exciting, getting to see and chat with the stars mingling before us or finally laying eyes on the movie and seeing myself on the IMAX screen with Tom Hanks! It was certainly the most surreal experience I could ever imagine!

In the end, I've been asked many times if I thought Flight 1549 was a "miracle," and I have to say without exaggeration: yes. While we were extremely lucky to have Captain Chesley Sullenberger at the controls for the world's only successful water ditching of a major airliner in aviation history, I find it quite miraculous that it was the first officer's very first trip, fresh out of training, which meant he was absolutely the sharpest and most proficient pilot Sully could have had sitting next to him, ready to run checklists and be able to offer apt assistance. And that, as they glided like a rock to the watery runway beneath them, they would miss the George Washington Bridge by only 800 feet. And that the airplane not only remained intact after the water impact, but that the airframe would remain afloat with all those passengers standing on its wings, even though when the fuselage was raised from the river it revealed a gash in the bulkhead so deep and wide that why it floated at all was completely astounding to even the structural engineers on scene. And that there were not one, not two, but three ferry boats converging near their splashdown spot who were able to begin rescuing passengers within five minutes. And that in the end, as one passenger remarked to me, from the time the event started until he was safely back on shore talking to his wife on his cell phone, less than thirteen minutes had passed. Miraculous indeed!

Lori was hired by Piedmont Airlines in 1984. She became the Director of Flight Safety, an Airbus 320 Check Airman, and an FAA designee before becoming a chief pilot with American Airlines. Lori loves spending time with her husband at his airshows and with their grandchildren.

Lori with Lucy Young, Clint Eastwood, and the rest of the simulator crew.

Captain Lori Cline flying the simulator in the "Sully" movie.

Friends and Family

My Most Memorable Flight
by Terry London Rinehart

T he most memorable flight in my fifty-plus years of flying occurred while I was sitting in the back of an airplane on March 9, 2010. In the plush leather seat next to me, idly gazing out the window at the slow-moving landscape below, sat my ninety-year-old mother, Barbara Erickson London. Our son Justin and a PBS crew had seen us off at the San Jose Airport. Across from us in the small Citation Jet sat my husband, Bob, and one of my twin daughters, Lauren. We smiled excitedly at each other, acknowledging the magnitude of the moment. We were *en route* to Washington, D.C., as part of an Angel Flight Mission for Barbara to receive the Congressional Gold Medal from Congress as part of her service as a WASP (Women Airforce Service Pilots) during WWII. Glancing up towards the cockpit, the captain manipulated the throttles to set cruise power. She looked back at me at that moment and smiled. The captain of the Citation, carrying three generations of pilots, was my other twin daughter, Kelly.

A highly decorated civilian pilot during WWII, Barbara was one of the original 25 members of the Women's Auxiliary Ferrying Squadron (WAFS) and a WASP. She was the commander of the base in Long Beach, California, and the only WASP to receive the Air Medal. During her time as a WASP, Barbara flew almost every make and model of military aircraft, including the P-51 and B-17.

Kelly, who was licensed to fly the jet as a single pilot, was able to have her twin sister join her in the cockpit. Lauren is also a rated pilot, so as I sat looking at the cockpit of the Citation, I saw my twin daughters at the controls. I could not have been more proud than I was that day, seeing my daughters flying my mother on what would be her last airplane ride.

I grew up surrounded by aviation. My father and mother were both pilots, and my father's brother was the first American Ace in Europe in a P-47. We always seemed to have access to an airplane even though we never owned one. My sister and I spent a lot of our childhood riding in the back of all different kinds of airplanes. When I turned sixteen and got my driver's license, it just seemed normal to get a job at the airport. I learned to fly while washing airplanes and answering the phone at a flight school in Long Beach, California. I reached my career goal of being an airline pilot when Western Airlines hired me in 1976. I spent twenty-eight years as an airline pilot and retired as a 767 captain for Delta Air Lines after Western Airlines was acquired by Delta in 1987. After retiring from Delta, I was fortunate enough to be hired by a private company to fly their Boeing 767 around the world for another seven years. All of my success in aviation can be attributed to the mentoring from my parents and the many others that went before me in aviation. Now I am happy to say that all three of my children are pilots, and they have children of their own that love flying. The legacy continues.

Terry London Rinehart was hired by Western Airlines in 1976 and retired from Delta Air Lines in 2005 as a Boeing 767 captain. In the seven years that followed her retirement, Terry flew a private 757/767 worldwide. Now she truly enjoys babysitting her grandchildren and flying the family airplane.

Kelly, Lauren, Barbara, and Terry in Washington, D.C.

A Story of a Friendship
by Margaret (Brewer) Bruce and
Denise Lonean Blankinship

S ometimes it seems that random decisions turn out to be responsible for one's life making a fortunate turn. That's how it was for me.

I had been feeling somewhat isolated. I didn't know any other women who were flying, but I knew they were out there. I first learned of ISA+21 from Karen Kahn, an original ISA member (there were twenty-one at the first convention) whose name had been given to me by a uniform tailor in Los Angeles. I was living in LA while flying as a DC-8 flight engineer for Pacific East Air, a child of deregulation. That was in 1983, and the annual ISA convention was to be in Seattle.

Another component of happenstance was my having chosen the Florida panhandle for a vacation with a good friend from the old days. Vacation over, I was coming out of Atlanta, begging a jumpseat on Eastern, headed to Seattle and my first ISA convention. By 1983 I was flying DC-8 as first officer for

Connie Kalitta, and Eastern was pretty much the only major who'd give us a jumpseat, as the airline world hadn't yet heard much about former racecar driver Connie Kalitta.

It was such a surprise that in May 1983, two hours after boarding that Eastern Airlines flight to Seattle, I met Denise Blankinship, as well as her mother Carla and another Piedmont pilot, Nancy (Moye) Law, who were all traveling together on the flight and going to ISA! They embraced me into their lives like a long-lost sister. In the hours from Atlanta to Seattle, I came to find Denise to be so real and warm and generous. Little did I know, she and I would fly together at Piedmont/ USAir/US Airways/American and, moreover, that we would become close friends for over thirty-five years.

Denise Blankinship is another original ISA Charter Member. A 737 captain with Piedmont Airlines, she was the second woman hired there. Over the USA skies, Denise was one of the very first female airline pilot voices on the ATC frequencies. In the late 1970s, while I was in California in college and just learning to fly, I had seen Denise Blankinship's picture on the front cover of "Flying Magazine." Denise had been the Georgia Flight Instructor of the Year, and she was also the second woman hired at Piedmont Airlines, and the first female 737 airline jet captain in the US. Oh, I had thought she was an unapproachable, high-level diva Goddess of Flying.

Denise knew everyone—she always knows everyone—and Denise took me under her wing. Piedmont was still small. I think she told someone, "Hey, if you're gonna hire girls, how about hiring one I like?" It must have helped. I was the twenty-first female pilot on the seniority list at Piedmont, and thanks to the stellar professional work of the twenty women who preceded me—including Denise, Cheryl Peters, Maggie (Rose) Badaracco, Valerie Wells, Nancy Law, Debbie Dubose, and Terrie Foote—I was met with an odd welcome by the male pilots: "Yeah, minority hiring. . . women? We got lotsa women, they're okay, but you're our first California Yankee."

As the next years unfolded at Piedmont, Denise and I flew together every few months or so, and, especially back then, it was very unusual for the captain and first officer to both be women, so of course people were startled. I remember one year on Valentine's Day, the weather was snowy-slushy-dreadful, and the plane was delayed inbound, so consequently, this last flight of the night was delayed outbound. When we boarded, the passengers boarded right on our heels. I was already in my seat when a man got on, saw Denise at the cockpit door in her hat and stripes, and said, "Oh no! A woman pilot! You're flying the plane? Are you sure you know what you're doing?"

Denise, in her distinctive south Georgia drawl, replied, "Well, sir, if you feel uncomfortable, maybe you'd feel better meeting my first officer—hey, Margaret, get on up here!" An hour later, Denise made the most beautiful landing on a short, slippery and snowy mountaintop runway at midnight in Charleston, West Virginia. Happy Valentine's Day!

Back in those days I had big curly "Flashdance" hair. On another 737 flight, a boarding passenger popped his head into the cockpit. "Excuse me," he said. I turned around, and he said, "Oh, good, a woman. I thought a hippie was flying the plane."

I always chuckle when remembering a sweet older southern lady at the cockpit door wearing a hat with a flower. She looked at our panel and said, "Will you look at all those clocks! Do you look at all those clocks at the same time?" I answered, "No, ma'am. Just one at a time."

Sometimes hopeful jumpseaters would come bearing gifts, and one Christmas a commuting TWA flight attendant presented Denise and me with a five-*pound* box of Godiva chocolates. You're on, Girlfriend! Two legs later, an Eastern Airlines pilot sat up in the cockpit because the cabin had filled up. He spied the Godiva Chocolates. "Sure, go ahead," Denise offered. Well, he ate a few chocolates but forgot to put the top back on the box. When we landed and pulled reverse, the box of Godiva chocolates slid forward and spilled all over the floor. "Oh, I'm so sorry," he muttered while plucking up the chocolates. We stared silently at the chocolates as he deposited them into the trash bag. Then he left. Not two seconds later, Denise and I popped up our heads and looked at each other like two gophers coming out of the ground. Both of us pounced on the trash bag, retrieved the Godiva morsels, brushed them off on our shirt sleeves, and then put them back in the box! That's thinking alike, I tell you. No germaphobes here. Those babies are ours! This is Godiva chocolate we're talking about!

While we are definitely friends, the job was always serious. With a high level of responsibility, it has to be. Denise was the captain and I was the first officer when on one cold day in October, Columbus Day, as I recall, we evacuated the airplane on the runway with a full flight—a seat in every seat. I bailed with the flight papers, the logbook, and the trash bag. By the way, that part they recommend in training about keeping people together? It is the truth. Passengers wander everywhere and that runway is a lot wider when you're standing ON it than when you're looking AT it.

Everyone knows where they were on 9/11. Denise and I were about to push back a 757 from Charlotte to Washington, D.C. We didn't get there, but instead parked that 757 on CLT Runway 23 nose to wingtip to tail with hundreds of other aircraft—Delta, KLM, Atlas, Avianca, British Airways, Southwest—that had all dropped into Charlotte on that sobering day. It wasn't until a week or so later that it occurred to me that we just might have had bad guys on our plane too. We never found out. Just luck.

Denise has enormous range. She gets along with so many people from so many corners of life. She can talk with anyone. She doesn't like to write, however. Always the captain, Denise pretty much deferred most paperwork to me. Even with the authoring of this article, Captain Denise again delegated "the paperwork" and asked me to write "our story." LOL. Gladly. Happy to do it.

Our friendship is a weave of the professional and the personal that spans more than three decades. My twins were born in 1994. Denise was at the hospital. She called in sick, I think. Plus, Denise is the twins' godmother. Good choice, I might add.

Over the years, Denise and I flew together on the 737 and later to the Caribbean and Europe on the 757 and 767, until I checked out on the 757 myself. Just before going to ground school for my captain checkout, I picked up Denise's Paris trip. Silly story: Denise had our big Paris layover safari all organized—the fancy mustard shop, shoe store, fresh bread, a stop for lunch, and so on. We got tired after a long day and decided to take the Paris Metro back to the hotel. Directed by someone to a Metro station/stop that was part of some underground shopping mall, we finally located the complicated kiosk for the tickets and attempted to decipher the instructions. My high school French was rusty. Denise only speaks Southern. There was no one around until finally a lone monsieur walked by and I attempted to ask in fumbling French how to buy the Metro ticket. The gentlemanly man answered in English, "This is not a Metro station. You are at the entrance to a parking garage." Oh. (Don't tell anyone we fly jets.) We laughed for hours. Still do. Can ya believe it?

Now that I am close to retiring, I think back on how quickly time has grown wings. There are so many unsaid thank yous. So many little stories. So many wonderful times and, yes, a few scary moments. So many kind and generous people, and, yeah, a few, not so much. Without question, countless people have touched my life in so many ways. Friendships are born of respect and camaraderie and that spark of delight. Aviation careers bring us together as family. Male or female, we all are part of a tapestry. None of us got here alone. We were all helped and encouraged, or even warned, when needed. Be it a boot in the behind, a wink, or a hug. It all comes full circle in its way.

I have met so many wonderful women (and men) in this honored family of professional aviators who have helped me to grow. It has been my privilege to have had a rewarding career flying trusting passengers who are with us like Chaucer's Travelers—united by our common journey. Professionally, where we pilots are all on a similar journey where there are still not many women, ISA gives us gals a home, if you will. It is a home where we are understood and bonded on the same path.

I am also privileged to have met so many worthy, respected, and skilled women (and men) pilots, many of whom have become friends. I am proud and honored and grateful for the happenstance that allowed Denise Blankinship to be one of those friends for me. She was always a good soul. Still is. Always will be.

In recent years, because of a convoluted family calendar, I have been more of a satellite member of ISA; however, I believe deeply in the spirit of ISA in that I actively encourage and respect my colleagues, wherever they are in their flying. I value enormously our official and unofficial family network of professional women (and men) aviators. We are all family.

Now I am squinting at the sunset. Denise retired last year. Soon I myself will hand over my own little baton to a younger generation of pilots who are savvy and capable. Yes, we will be in good hands. As for me, I have so enjoyed a good career doing something I love. Blessed to have had my turn at the wheel, I'm sure glad it worked out that way.

So, thank you to happenstance and good fortune. And most of all, thank you, my friends! I couldn't have done it without you!

Margaret learned to fly airplanes and helicopters in California, and was hired by Piedmont Airlines in 1984. A rewarding airline career as an American Airlines 767 captain concluded with her retirement in May 2018. She intends the next chapter to include backpacking with her pilot husband, reinstating her CFI, and visiting her twenty-four-year-old twins who are both pilots.

Denise was hired by Piedmont Airlines in 1977. She retired at American in 2015 as captain on the Boeing 767. Captain Blankinship lives in Georgia and enjoys promoting health and fitness to friends and family.

Captain Denise Blankinship with Copilot Margaret Brewer Bruce.

A Great Friendship
by Jane McCaffery DeLisle

I remember being a new hire at Piedmont Airlines in 1989. I had come straight from flying corporate jets in a very small flight department where everyone knew everyone. When one of us moved, we all showed up to help; when someone had a birthday, we all celebrated. Now I was at Piedmont Airlines, which had about 3,000 pilots at that time. I was based in Charlotte, NC, where with the exception of my nine new hire male classmates based in Charlotte, I knew no one.

It was very intimidating every time I walked into the crew room. There were always a lot of older men, all reading, talking, doing their Jeppesen revisions, napping on sofas. I'd walk in and look to see a familiar face; there usually was never a person that I remotely knew. I *dreaded* walking into that crew room to sign in for my trip and get my flight bag. About the second or third month that I was there, a tall blond female pilot walked up to me and said, "Hey! I'm Denise Blankinship. I'm an old fart here." I was stunned! Here was another female pilot, and she was friendly! She told me that if I needed anything, to give her a call. She then wrote down her name and phone number on a scrap of paper and walked off. I looked down at the paper and was in awe! A captain, a female captain, talked to me and offered her help.

Well, that was almost twenty-eight years ago. Since then, we have seen each other through ups and downs. She welcomed me to my first ISA convention. I was a bridesmaid in her spectacular wedding; she met my new boyfriend, a fellow pilot who became my husband, twenty-six years ago. We have cheered each other through training and checkrides. Denise was one of the first people I called when my dad collapsed unexpectedly and we prayed together, and she called me as soon as she found out that her husband had died suddenly. She listened as I told her I was getting furloughed after working for Piedmont (now US Airways/American) for fourteen years. She wrote a letter of recommendation and got me an interview at another airline. She let me stay with her when I was recalled back to US Airways.

Yes, we have seen a lot of ups and downs, but we have gotten through this together as friends. Denise is one of my very best friends. I cherish the day she walked up to me and welcomed me to the group! I never had a sister, but if I could choose one, it would be Denise Blankinship.

In 1989 Jane was hired at USAir/Piedmont. She is currently flying captain and is a check airman with American Airlines. In her free time Jane loves to explore different countries with her husband Joe.

Denise Blankinship, Joe and Jane DeLisle,
Maggie Rose Badaracco.

Jane taking a selfie with ISA friends.

Love Story
by Becky Howell

When I was about eight years old, I took the book I was reading about "eagle-eyed pilots" to my dad and said, "I wanna be a PILOT when I grow up!"

His answer was, "I would be the last person to discourage you from whatever you want to do, but they don't let girls be pilots, and they don't let people with glasses be pilots, so I think you should choose a more realistic goal." (I was already wearing glasses.)

This was about 1960 when daddies were <u>always</u> right, so I threw the idea overboard.

While in high school, I worked in a pharmacy and decided, "I can do that." So I set my target at pharmacist.

While I was in Houston at pharmacy school, I learned to ride motorcycles. When the president of the club that I rode with was killed in a motorcycle accident, a bunch of the members and I became Motorcycle Safety Foundation (MSF) instructors. (Dick had been one of the first instructors trained in an experimental curriculum on motorcycle safety education that had been created and taught at Texas A&M University. We took the ball that he had pitched and ran with it.) *[A&M was my dad's Alma Mater and Mecca, as far as I was concerned. I was just sorry they didn't have a pharmacy school.]*

We created a subdivision of the state organization that we belonged to and taught classes on a volunteer basis statewide. After a couple of years of this, two of us were pretty tired of doing most of the work, so we decided to go to MSF and become Chief Instructors so that we could train more instructors and not have to work so hard. We did. We also helped write the state law that requires that minors take a motorcycle course before getting a license. Since the Texas legislature meets every other year, I figured that gave me a two-year window to have a larger and better organized operation than we were running at the time, and since a pharmacist didn't know a boatload about bureaucracy, I would take the GRE and go back to school to learn what I needed to know to head that organization. Texas A&M seemed like the best place to do that since they had created the curriculum (and I'd wanted to go there since birth—some of us really *are* born with maroon blood). I quit my pharmacy job and went to graduate school.

Now I have to back-track just a bit to weave in another subject. While I was practicing pharmacy, I had a salesman that would come around each month. Since he was a private pilot, a routine statement was, "As much as you like motorcycles, you'd LOVE FLYING!" To which my reply would be the girl and glasses story. He told me that he knew that they had fixed the girl "problem," but he wasn't sure about the glasses problem. We went through this routine for several months.

Then one day he said, "You could fly ultralights."

"What's that?"

"Well, it's a small aluminum frame with fabric wings and a motorcycle engine. It's a one-person airplane, and you don't have to have a license to fly it, so you won't need a medical and no one will care about the glasses."

"Where do I go to look at one?"

"Well... I don't know. They are so light that the winds must be almost calm to fly them. It's a little too windy for them here on the Gulf coast."

So I threw that idea overboard, too.

On my first day at A&M, strung across the walkway between Rudder and the MSC was an enormous banner, "ULTRALIGHT FLYING ORGANIZATION, FIRST MEETING, THURS. NIGHT, ROOM ###."

I've heard that word before. I'll go see what it's all about.

The graduate students that had created the club had already written the constitution and bylaws. They were some really far-sighted guys. They had also acquired from the administration a piece of turf near the polo field that could be used for take-offs and landings. Two of the other particularly smart moves were to require that the aircraft (when a kit was purchased and put together) be a 3-axis controlled plane (so that folks transitioning to "real" aircraft would not have developed bad habits) and that each member get five hours in a REAL airplane before flying the club plane—an attempt to not always be rebuilding the kit.

Of course there was no money at that point, but we kept a few of the 500 folks that showed up at that first meeting and began projects to save enough money to buy a kit. To set an example, I began the five hours of required flying. That instructor also knew *they* had solved the girl problem, but he didn't know about the glasses.

By the end of that semester I was president of that club (and of the motorcycle club). In the spring, the president of the skydiving club called me—they wanted to jump into our "turf" on Parents' Day. I told him that we didn't have an airplane yet, so we certainly wouldn't be in the way, but, for protocol, I would take it to the members for approval and that, in my opinion, he could consider it done.

After that conversation, it took him less than two sentences to talk me into jumping out of a "perfectly good" airplane. I had seen folks do that once before and wanted to try it. Did I have the courage to do that?

Back then (1983), the Aggies were travelling to Austin's Bird's Nest Airport to jump. So I became a student skydiver there. The fixed base operator (FBO) was (of course) a pretty long distance from the jump center and having been issued a one-hour bladder, I was over there pretty often, or making the trek between the two. So I became pretty familiar with the faces of some of the airport locals that were not skydivers.

There was the guy that seemed to run the FBO/Airport—probably owned the place, too. The mechanic. A few pilots who came around often enough for me to recognize faces. And usually if two or more of these folks were together, there were wonderful "hangar" flying stories to listen to, most of them funny ones! Occasionally, if I didn't have to be right back at the jump center, I hung around and eavesdropped.

That spring, my birthday was on a Monday. (Birthdays are *very special* to me because my uncle's *first words* to my mother were, "You'll never raise her." He was trying to prepare her for my death. I was too small and weak and did, in fact, nearly die twice before we left the hospital and quite a few times since then.) My mom and stepfather had come out to the drop zone (DZ) to bring me my favorite pie (green grape) and a card with a little money in it. But then they left. After all, golf *is* more important than watching your oldest daughter jump out of a perfectly good airplane.

So I put my presents away and headed for the FBO. On the way there, I saw, out in front of the maintenance hangar, a small airplane (later identified as a Tri-Pacer) being washed by the mechanic. Two other guys (one was a local pilot that I recognized and the other was someone I'd never seen before) were standing there with their arms folded across their chests, *watching* him wash the airplane. All three looked very bored.

As I walked by, I had a big grin on my face (from the pre-birthday visit), so the tallest guy (the local pilot) with his arms folded, said, "What are YOU so happy about?"

"Tomorrow's my birthday!"

"Well, *today's* mine, do I get anything?"

"Happy Birthday!" So I gave him a hug and he stole a kiss. I went on about my business.

A few weeks later I had made the usual potty run and was hanging around the FBO listening to funny flying stories for as long as I could, but, as I had a jump coming up, I needed to leave for the dirt dive. As I headed for the door, the tall guy asked if he could walk me back to the drop zone.

"Sure," I said and lit off at my normal pace (which is pretty fast—Dad was tall and didn't slow down for us when we were young). He didn't seem to have any trouble keeping up with me, but that was before I noticed whether or not I needed to slow down for folks. He began what appeared to be asking me out.

"Buh, dee bah duh, duh."

You could see him restart his mental computer. He tried again. "Buh, dee bah duh, duh, *PIZZA!*"

I laughed. "I think I got the message. I can't go tonight, but if you'll ask me again, I will go out with you."

In the blink of an eye, he nodded his head, did a 180° turn and left.

I chuckled to myself all the way back to the DZ.

A few weeks later he got up the nerve to ask me out again, and we went to dinner. During our dinner conversation, I learned that he was a commercial pilot and flew a Cessna 421 from Austin for a local corporation. But he wore glasses that were *very* thick.

So I asked him to let me see his glasses. He was puzzled. "Sure." While he took them off, I took my contacts out and left them there on the table. I tried on his glasses. Hmm. . . almost. I turned them upside down so that the left lens was now over my right eye—perfect! His glasses were exactly the same as mine! We had the same vision, but in opposite eyes! But...how can *you* fly and not me?

He explained the waiver program for folks with serious glasses. (A student pilot could get a 3rd class medical with whatever glasses they had, so long as they could see well enough to pass. For a commercial medical with vision worse than 20/100, you had to see a special ophthalmologist for a complete evaluation. The doctor I went to in San Antonio was also an aero medical examiner, so he could do all of the other required tests and send the evaluation to the FAA for a decision on issuance of a special certificate of demonstrated ability (also known as a waiver). Corrected to 20/20 is all that's required now that the regs have changed.

That summer we traded motorcycle lessons for flying lessons and fell in love in the process. By fall my mom still had not come back to the DZ to see me jump, so I got the idea of taking the skydive to her.

She lived in the country. We could rent an airplane and fly over her house. I could jump in for Thanksgiving, and David could land in the pasture across the highway. We could have dinner with them and then head back to Austin. To keep it a secret, I colluded with my brother-in-law, Jeff. The entire family would be at Mom's this Thanksgiving. We would fly

over the house and circle back on jump run. When he heard
the airplane overhead, he was to round everyone up and get
them out into the front yard.

[A couple of weeks before this jump, I went to a seminar
to learn to do Canopy Relative Work—stacking canopies one
on top of the other in formation. Since I was the only girl
there (lightweight), I had to re-trim my parachute for maximum forward drive to be able to catch the guys' faster driving
parachutes. This had changed the stall angle of attack on my
parachute to a point where when using the brakes, it would
stall earlier than on all previous jumps. After that training day,
I made only a couple more jumps at this new configuration.]

I stuffed the baggy legs of my jumpsuit with Hershey's
Kisses for the kids. After I bailed out on jump run, I ripped
open the Velcro and down they fell. Beautiful! Shining silver
bits fluttering into the yard. The kids and adults loved it!

As I got near my landing area, I realized that I had more
drive than I wanted. Mom's house was on a hill. The wind
was from the south (and I had calculated a *perfect* exit point
for *flat* land), and the front yard was on the NORTH (downwind) side of the house!

I immediately went to the arm position that would
have given me full brakes (like full flaps). Only now it was
full *STALL!*

My canopy collapsed at about 50 feet (depending on who
you talk to). I dropped like a rock into Mom's yard. A perfect
butt strike! *CRACK!* My canopy re-inflated and settled between
me and my little crowd who were now running toward me
in horror. That gave me time to wiggle my feet and see if the
message still got delivered. Good!

I tried to talk Lisa (my middle sister) through field-packing
the parachute. I knew I had hurt myself pretty badly but that
someday I'd get back to jumping, and I did not want to have

to untangle everything when that time came. No good. She was too flustered to follow instructions well.

"OK. I'm gonna keep my body straight, like I'm on a board. Y'all lift me and rotate me around my ankles so that I can stand up."

"Now, hand me the parachute." I field-packed it and gave it back to her. Then I got Mom and Valorie (baby sis) under my arms and we walked up to the house. "OK. Lay me down (on the living room floor) just like you got me up. If I feel this bad in an hour, you can take me to the hospital." At 30 minutes, I was ready to be taken to the car. "Tell me when you're ready for me."

They started unloading golf clubs and other stuff from the back of the Wagoneer. Someone (I think it was Jeff, but I don't really remember) came in and told me they were ready a few minutes *too* early. We did the stand-up trick again, and I walked outside supported in the same fashion as before. They leaned me up against another vehicle to finish the unloading. I got dizzy. (I had low blood pressure, so getting dizzy just meant putting my head between my legs till it passed.) *OUCH! That hurt!*

That spurred them to act faster and soon I was rolled into the back of the Jeep. We lurched off to town and X-rays. Jim Price, the physician that has been in on nearly all of my accidental attempts to extricate myself from this life, met us there and X-rayed me. He came back in and said, "I guess you know you broke it." "Yup. How bad?" "Simple compression fracture, L-3. I don't think you'll even need traction, but I want the orthopod to see you on Monday or Tuesday when he's back at work. I'm going to put you in the hospital here for now."

So I spent Thanksgiving in the hospital. Ten days' worth. No traction, no plaster. Just lying there. Everything hurt.

After they released me from the hospital (I still couldn't walk), I moved in with Mom and Sox. I had already called A&M and said that I wouldn't be able to finish the semester (we only had one more week left) and negotiated for grades. Seniors and grad students in their last semester don't have to take finals. You just get your course grade. I had one course where the ONLY grade for the semester was going to be a project, so that prof decided it would be unfair to my teammates if he gave me an A that *they* had to "work" for. He gave me a B. It didn't phase him that I had been our team leader and had done most of the work on our project. (In retaliation for being admitted to A&M on probation, I had planned to graduate with all As.)

I called the graduation office. "I really want to come to graduation, but I have a problem—I can't walk. In fact, I can't even sit yet. But if I can teach myself to walk before the ceremony, can you stick me on something flat somewhere out of sight and let me know a few names in advance of mine so I can get up, receive my diploma, then duck out the back door?"

"Sure! We'll use a gurney from the PE department, and there's a little foyer near the stage. You'll even be able to see what's going on! You just come to this door when you get here, and good luck learning how to walk!"

I did it. I taught myself to walk again through the pain. Then I began extending my distances to total what I figured I'd have to cover to get out of the building. We all gathered up and went to A&M.

The gurney was ready for me. The "out of the way" foyer... *well, ONLY 3/4 of the folks in G. Rolley White Coliseum could see me!* AND they were all pointing at me and saying things like, "What's she doing down there...?"

The graduation went well, and I scooted out the back door of the auditorium and waited *forever* for them to come pick me up. David had to park a very long way from the coliseum after he let us out.

After that, David and Sebesta moved my stuff from the house in Bryan that I had shared with Pat Martin to David's house. I moved in with him with a broken back! He had already been through the "sickness" part and passed with flying colors!

Today we've been together for 33+ years (2016). We still have had only one argument: Who got the best deal? And we both still think we won the grand prize!

He finished teaching me to fly alternately in the Cessna 150 and the 421. In fact, on my third 421 lesson, he had me flying on instruments in a snowstorm. I got my private rating. Then we bought a C-172, and I got my commercial and instrument ratings in that airplane. I got my multi-engine rating before I got my instrument and began logging flying time with him in the C-421. I was doing all the flying and his boss really liked me (not to mention having two pilots for the price of one). There never was any question about whether or not I *could* do something; instead, it was, "OK, what do I do now?"

We now have 297 acres that we have turned into a residential airport. We live in a trailer house that we gutted; then he rebuilt all of the interior. We have a really nice house on the inside of that frame. The airport is our life-long project.

There are many other stories along the way of our relationship, but that's how one goes from being a pharmacist to a major airline pilot in only eight years. Southwest is my fifth airline, and I will be forced to retire from them in the spring of 2017 due to FAA age limits (discrimination).

Three years ago I went through over a year of treatment for and recovery from triple negative breast cancer (a very rare form of breast cancer). Now David is fighting non-Hodgkin's lymphoma, diffuse large B-cell, double hit. That fight has been going on for over eight months, with three different chemo

regimens and radiation so far. We're hoping to find a bone mar-
row donor or to get him into an immunotherapy clinical trial,
but we haven't heard anything from either of those in weeks.

Becky began working for Southwest Airlines in 1991 and retired as a captain in 2017. Her mate, David, died in March of 2017 from a rare cancer seven weeks before her retirement. Becky now spends her time working on both her airport and her cattle ranch in Texas.

Captain Becky Howell's retirement flight
with ISA+21 member, Chris Beltran.

Becky's David enjoying their cat's antics.

Two Memorable Flights
by Tammy Blakey

I have been an airline pilot for over 34 years and a captain for 31 of those years. There have been many different situations I have dealt with, including unruly passengers, medical emergencies, mechanical problems, etc. One event that happened only once in my career was flying former President George H.W. Bush from Narita, Japan, to Houston, Texas, in 2000.

There were four pilots on this international flight on the Boeing 777. We had decided to flip to see who would fly the flight and land the plane. I won the toss. The most surprising thing about the flight, to me, was how quickly we received our clearance and requested altitude from the controllers in Japan. For those of you who have flown internationally, you probably remember how rare that was, as JAL (Japanese Airlines) was always given altitude priority. Everyone from the ground crew to controllers must have known who we had on board. Of course, President Bush didn't go through security like most people, he just came up to the side of the plane in a black SUV with his security team. They deplaned the same way after we parked at the gate in Houston.

In the middle of the flight President Bush asked to come up to the flight deck. He was wearing slippers with the presidential seal on them and one of the first officers asked him how one gets a pair of slippers with the seal on them. He jokingly replied, "You get elected President." President Bush talked fondly of his wife Barbara and chatted about the flight for about a half an hour with us; he then gave us each a tie tack with the Presidential seal on it.

Another event occurred more recently while flying the new Boeing 787 from Los Angeles to Melbourne, Australia. It comes to mind because I had never had so many passengers shake my hand and thank me for flying a flight.

I was taxiing the aircraft out for takeoff when about 200 feet from the runway, I smelled something kind of funny. There was a slight chemical smell to it. The other pilots didn't smell it. I asked the relief pilot seated behind me, to call the flight attendants to see if they were cooking anything in the ovens. The flight attendant informed us they weren't cooking anything, but there was a haze in the cabin. I made the decision to go back to the gate and have all of the passengers deplane. A maintenance team came on board. They discovered that a recirculation fan had caught on fire and had done some damage below the flight deck. The flight was cancelled as there wasn't another B-787 available.

Any time a flight cancels it ends up being a pretty big deal as 252 passengers have to be put up in hotels and rebooked on another flight. As it ended up, my crew and I were sent to a hotel in Los Angeles as well and flew the same passengers the following evening to Melbourne. In my announcement to the passengers the next evening, I told them about the fire in the lower part of the aircraft, and that it ended up to being a very good thing we didn't takeoff the night before. Virtually every passenger thanked me as they deplaned in Melbourne. I was expecting to get some complaints about our late arrival, but I did not receive one complaint about arriving in Melbourne a day late.

Tammy was hired by Continental in 1984 as a second officer on the Boeing B727. She flies as a captain on the Boeing 787 for United Airlines. Tammy and her family raise cattle and horses on their ranch in Washington State.

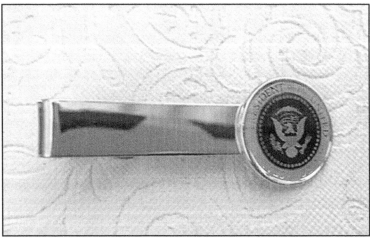

From Manure to Blue Skies
by Judy Lee

I was a bit of a wild weed growing up, not having a specific direction or idea of what I wanted to do when I "grew up." I rode and showed horses from the time I was very young, so young that I don't remember exactly when I started, so I naturally thought the equestrian life would be my future. Then reality hit when I was in college and I was supposed to pick a "major" for the "grown-up" chapter in life. My mother, a veteran of WWII, told me I could be a nurse, as she was, a teacher, or a secretary. My father, also a veteran of the Army Corps of Engineers, and a man ahead of his time, told me I could be a contractor, as he was, or do anything else I wanted to do. Having worked summer jobs, I knew I did not want a nine-to-five job in an office without the smell of horses. I spent two semesters in Florence, Italy, for my junior year in the early '70s and, as fate would have it, on my way home from Europe, I met a jockey who invited me to the races the next day.

My parents couldn't believe I would spend my first day home at the track but reluctantly agreed to let me go. That afternoon, I crossed paths with a horse trainer who I had met at the local airport a year or so before. We had aviation and horses in common so we became fast friends. He introduced me to another trainer who needed exercise riders. My first job on the track started a few days later! That led to four-plus years on the track, traveling around the country, "galloping" these magnificent animals in their morning workouts. I loved the people, many of whom were characters right out of Horatio Alger books; I loved the daily work, the smell of manure, waking early to be at the barn by 5:30 a.m., going to the races in the afternoon, and traveling from the East Coast tracks to the Midwest to California tracks, dedicating myself to this life. I thought this would be my life's work, in some capacity. I was fortunate to be a natural lightweight at 100 pounds, so I thought I would try to be a jockey. I was fortunate to ride some training races and exhibition races, but I never got my jockey's license, which put me on another path, one that I would maintain for over four decades.

While I loved those four years with the race horses, I continued my general aviation flying, thinking there must be something in aviation that I could do as a profession. I had started flying in 1970, thinking I only wanted to be a private pilot and fly for fun. I had already been told by the military when they came to my university, recruiting for the Vietnam War that they would NEVER EVER have women flying their aircraft. That was 1971. And I knew the airlines weren't planning to hire women because my flight instructor told me so! I already had my private, commercial, and instrument rating so it was mostly just fun flying on the East Coast. One of the West Coast horse owners had a King Air and a personal pilot who allowed me to fly right seat whenever schedules allowed. This wonderful man encouraged me to continue flying, believing aviation would eventually open its doors to women.

I didn't have a mentor or know many professional pilots who encouraged me to do anything in aviation, but I did have the most wonderful, supportive father who always told me growing up that I could do whatever I wanted, even if it wasn't a traditional job for women. His words have lived on in my brain my entire life. He was the first and only person who would fly around in a Cessna 150 with me when I initially got my private pilot's license. Did I mention he was very brave? The only other passenger who would go on adventures with me in the early days was my beautiful German Shepherd companion, Killer. She loved to fly, which made my dad very happy since it relieved him of experiencing the terror a low-time pilot must cause non-aviators.

I continued to gallop horses on the track while I worked on my CFII and multiengine ratings, and then instructed and flew Part 135. So I worked at the track in the mornings and flew in the afternoons and evenings. That was my life, seven days a week on the track and six days flying. Bonnie Tiburzi was one of my early friends in aviation, so when she was hired in 1973 by American Airlines, it dawned on me that the airlines may indeed hire more women in the future. That was when I dug my heels in and started working toward a goal.

I was in the right place at the right time and had applications in to all the airlines. I remember Eastern Airlines only wanting to send me an application to be a flight attendant and Pan Am very nicely, but in no uncertain terms, telling me they would NEVER hire women pilots. At the time, there were less than a handful of "regional carriers." In the summer of 1977, I received a letter from United Airlines inviting me to an initial interview, which would be in September. It was a long process of various interviews, testing (including the Stanine test, used in the Air Force for officer candidates), medicals, and simulator rides. I was hired in early 1978 for an April third class date.

I felt incredibly lucky to be hired as "Chick 5" and to follow our first female, Gail Gorski, who set a very professional example for the rest of us. It was a time when there were so few women with the airlines that if we saw one another at any airport, we would dash across terminals to meet. Thanks go to Beverley Bass and Stephanie Wallach for starting ISA in 1978, which would eventually bring many of us together to form friendships lasting many decades. I could not have gotten through the toughest times without my girlfriends, especially Sydney Hale; we shared each other's experiences with a common bond that no one else could understand. We met as flight instructors in 1976 and have had each other's backs for over four decades.

I had a very supportive new hire class. There were a total of eight of us, and we bonded quickly over dinners and studying. My first bid was a Boeing 727 engineer or second officer; however, I was assigned to be a "GIB" on the B-737. A "Guy in the Back" on the B-737 was a pseudo flight engineer. I bid to the B-727 before I was even out of school, so I only spent three months as a GIB. It was a time before political correctness, and I knew we women were under the microscope. Sometimes it was tough to decide if it was okay to joke with the guys or maintain that strict professional behavior. So I developed my own rule of three: be SOP (Standard Operating Procedures), be professional, and be cool. It helped me throughout my career because early attitudes ranged from one captain telling me he would do everything he could to get me fired and throwing the hard-plastic card with takeoff performance data at my neck, to another captain with a twelve-year-old daughter (Mary) who included me in dinners with other pilots while we all sat on reserve, reassuring me that I had their support. Another captain had a large bouquet of flowers on the desk of my engineer's panel when I showed up to work early one morning. They seemed to either love us or hate us. By the way, that captain with the twelve-year-old daughter would celebrate her being hired by United in 1989! Furthermore, Mary flew with me on my retirement flight on the B-777 in 2016!

My time with United included over 20 years of ALPA union work in various positions, with my favorite having been my position as MEC Chair of our Professional Standards Committee when we merged with Continental Airlines. No one wanted the merger, including me, but once I started working with my counterparts from the CAL Professional Standards Committee, my whole attitude changed. They had a stellar committee who wanted the same things the legacy UAL committee wanted. Since we had little help from our management at the time, it was really up to the pilots to work together internally and maintain a safe operation. I loved being a part of the integration process and being the first committee to completely integrate without any negative issues at all. Meeting Pam Perdue and joining her UAL Venus List on Facebook for LCAL and LUAL women not only improved my attitude further but is the reason I became such a strong proponent of a harmonious integration. I credit Pam with doing more as an individual than anyone else at the new United Airlines in bringing our women together and helping soothe the hard feelings the integration would inevitably bring.

I also worked in the Los Angeles flight office for a while following 9/11 and appreciated the opportunity to help rebuild a very sad pilot group to get the airline up and running again. My sense of duty comes from my parents, who proudly served our country in desperate times. While I did not serve in the military, I did my best to serve my fellow pilots and other employees. I loved my job, despite strikes by the pilots and mechanics, a two-year furlough, deregulation, bankruptcy, merger and the crazy 38+ year ride of roller coaster proportions. I was lucky to live in domicile and be able to stay senior, have a family, and retire. The changes I've seen in aviation since I started with the airlines in 1978 have been more dramatic than I could have imagined. My advice to young aviators is to savor every day of good health and enjoy every trip—even the difficult ones, and always stay with your passions and believe in yourself.

Judy was hired by United in 1978 as a second officer on the Boeing 727. She retired in 2016 as a captain on the Boeing 777. Judy volunteers, takes a variety of classes and goes to Jack Russell Terrier trials with her dog Peanut, and loves spending time with her two sons and daughters-in-law.

Mary Berlingeri-Meade (short hair), Judy Lee, and Missy Hohnstein Phillips on the ramp with a photobomber.

Judy, Mary, and Missy

How I Met My Husband
by Jane Saddler

I was visiting my sister in Juneau, Alaska, having flown up from my American Airlines base in Dallas, where I was an MD-80 first officer. Upon my departure, I awaited the arrival of the Alaska Airlines 737-400 on which I planned to jumpseat to Seattle. The Juneau operations office is located in the old airport control tower, commanding a fine view of the airport and surrounding mountains, glaciers, and sea, although that day we had typical winter weather for Southeast Alaska—low ceilings, poor visibility, rain, high winds, and absolute minimums for landing, compounded with short runways and forbidding terrain. After the aircraft arrived, the operations agent and I waited for the captain to climb up to ops to receive his briefing for the next leg of his flight. We waited and waited, and finally the agent told me that I'd better get down to the jet because they would be closing it out soon. When I entered the cockpit, the captain was still sitting in his seat, not having moved since landing. He had been challenged during the arriving flight, as he had been on few previous flights in the Navy, in his duty as a carrier attack pilot, and then at Alaska. He needed time to recuperate from all the considerations we airline pilots juggle each flight—weather, alternates, fuel, options, terrain—and was in the exhausted state of mind we all can identify with. I asked, "Captain, may I please ride your jumpseat to Seattle?" He gazed back at me and said, "Yes, if you'll marry me."

That, at least, is his side of the story.

I learned en route to Seattle that he had flown twelve years on the 727 as second officer, first officer, and captain, flying round dial throughout Alaska, and that he was painfully adjusting from the 3-pilot, 3-engine 727 to the new electronic 737 with a mere two engines and two pilots, this being his first winter on his new aircraft. This handsome, friendly, intelligent pilot regaled me with every detail of his new aircraft, and I remember that he was, after a lifetime of dodging aspiring love interests, a tough nut to crack. Some days after we landed in Seattle, he sent me a note through American company mail, ever the frugal airline pilot not wanting to spend a stamp on the U.S. Mail, inviting me to look him up if I ever bid a Seattle layover. Well, "natch," I bid a line of Seattle layovers, but they were all-nighters. One night, though, I flew a Kansas City turn from Dallas which was followed by a late-night Seattle flight. Midwest thunderstorms delayed our Kansas City turn so when I returned to Dallas, I had mere minutes to make my Seattle flight; I ran to the gate and booted out the reserve who had been called to replace me. I explained to the guy I was flying with that I had a hot 24-hour date in Seattle and didn't want to misconnect. He told me that the man I was flying to see was GU, to which I replied, "What's GU?" Geographically undesirable, it turns out. Au contraire. I convinced this Alaska pilot and Seattle resident that we could make beautiful music—er—children together, and now we have two boys and one girl, the oldest of whom is a private pilot with instrument rating, working on his commercial license, and we have enjoyed twenty years of marital bliss.

That, at least, is my side of the story.

Jane was hired in 1991 at American Airlines as a flight engineer on the Boeing 727. She retired in 2018 as captain on the Boeing 777, also having flown the McDonnell Douglas MD-80. Jane lives in Seattle and enjoys family ski trips.

Jane and Bruce Saddler and their three children.

Timing is Everything
by Tracy Prior Welch

I t was 1974, I was twelve years old, and my father, Freeman Garver Prior, an airline pilot with United Airlines, took me up in a C-172 at the Leesburg airport, Virginia. "Did you like it?" he asked. After responding yes, he said, "Okay. When you are 16 and can drive yourself to the airport, I'll pay for your flying lessons." And he did.

At twelve years old, I no longer contemplated a career as a Rockette, dancing in New York, or becoming a stewardess like my mother. Instead, my focus was on becoming an airline pilot like my father. After all, Dad liked his job, and we got to travel. He made good money, he was home all the time, and he didn't have any homework. Who wouldn't like that? Mom thought it was a good idea to have a goal, which was great advice. It gave me focus, and decisions were simply based around reaching the goal. My high school yearbook said I was going to become an airline pilot, and I did.

How lucky to grow up in a home knowing I could do whatever I wanted and have the parental emotional and financial support. Timing was right. I was grateful. My parents were forward-thinking in suggesting an airline career. After all, in 1974, women were just then beginning to pave the way in airline and military aviation careers. A very select few women were being hired by airlines and getting military flying slots again since the WASPs in WWII. At the time I did not know it was unusual for a woman to pursue an airline career. I just pressed on with my goal to be an airline pilot because I wanted the career, and no one told me otherwise. Years later a passenger brought her daughter to the cockpit to see the lady captain and tell her daughter that girls could be pilots, too. What did she mean "too"? I never realized women couldn't be pilots.

Dad's background was as a naval aviator. While a finance major at Duke, he joined the navy at the end of WWII. When the war ended, he finished up his degree, became a banker and joined the navy reserves. At 30 years old, he quit banking and became a pilot with Capital Airlines. Eventually Capital merged with United Airlines, and he later retired from both the Navy and United Airlines. He quit flying in the reserves in 1962, the year I was born. He told me he quit flying low over the Atlantic Ocean looking for German submarines because he had a little girl at home. Of course, his world revolved around me! Little did I know the Naval Air Station Anacostia had shut down to fixed-wing aircraft in 1962. Again, timing.

Capital is where my father met my mom, Leila Ruth Hillenbach. She was flight attendant, then called hostess, and was 14 years his junior. Some would jest he left a wife for a young hostess. Having been fiscally conservative, he would respond that he skipped the first wife and waited for the second one to come along.

Mom had to quit her job when she married in 1959 because at the time airline hostesses could not be married. Mom was always ahead of her time. She soloed a plane when she was younger, had been an All-State in high school basketball, attended Girls' State in NJ, and went to Colby College a year before attending Georgetown's Foreign Service School. For the first time, women could live on campus and were housed in the new nurse's dorm. After a year at Georgetown, she realized the women were being groomed for secretaries, not ambassadors, so she quit to be an airline hostess and travel. Always grateful and never complaining, she took the path the times dictated.

Why was my dad so progressive? My father had progressive parents—both were ahead of their time. Born in 1892, my grandmother U. Louise Garver was a graduate of Vassar University and worked in D.C. after WWI. When younger, she took tennis lessons, until her father told her women did not do that. She could always imagine the movement of her arm and the swish of the racket and resented not being able to play. Once married, she was in a progressive relationship where her husband did the cooking. Before she was married, she always wanted to be a pilot. As a young woman, she was in love with a pilot who was killed in a plane crash and she was heartbroken. I have a photograph on my dresser of my grandmother, standing by a Canadian Curtis plane on November, 15, 1919 in Washington, D.C., after she had gone for a 30-minute ride and did a 90-degree spiral. It cost $15 for 15 minutes. It wasn't until recently that I read the back of the photo and realized the pilot who took her flying was the famed aviator E. Hamilton Lee, "the flyingest man in the world," quoted as saying, "There are old pilots and bold pilots, but there are no old, bold pilots." While she never became a pilot, both of her sons became pilots, as did two of her grandchildren. Grandmother's advice was that you only regret the things in life that you do not do. She also commented that she was born ahead of her time.

My father said the three most important components about the airline career were seniority, seniority, and seniority. So the earlier I could be hired, the faster I would move up the seniority list and increase my quality of life later in the career. With that advice, I wanted to get my ratings and build my flight time as quickly as possible.

So at 16, when I could drive myself to the airport, I took flying lessons. While I lived and went to high school in Vienna, VA, I took ground school at the local community college, flight lessons at Colgan Airways in Manassas, VA, and earned my pilot's license before attending Salem College, WV, in 1979. As a career aviation major, earning a Bachelor's degree along with my instrument rating, commercial license, and certified flight instructor and instrument instructor licenses, I graduated in three years at 20 years old. In my senior year, I taught a ground school and flight instructed. As graduation approached, I called military guard units about a flying job, but was told women could not fly fighters nor fly transport airplanes because they went into combat zones, and the only unit that would consider a female pilot were the hurricane hunters. Having been taught to stay away from bad weather, I passed on that option. Timing was not quite right for the military, but the civilian route proved to be a quicker trek to the desired airline job anyway.

Spring break of my senior year I went to the eastern shore and traveled airport to airport with my resume to line up a summer flying job. I was hired by Garrison Aviation at a grass strip in Rehoboth Beach, DE, to fly aerial advertising banners up and down the beach. Not only did I fly them, I went merchant to merchant selling them. Besides banner towing, I gave sightseeing rides and flight instructed. Come winter when the operation slowed down, I was approached to run a flight school for Resort Airlines in Ocean City, MD. While I still gave sightseeing rides and flight instructed, I added charter flying to my resumé as well and earned my multi-engine rating. I was the first woman to fly for both Garrison and Resort Aviation. The next year, I went back to Manassas, VA, where Colgan Airways hired me to fly a single engine chase plane behind their Beach-99. I carried the golf clubs that did not fit into the B-99 to Hot Springs, VA, the highest commercially served airport east of the Mississippi. It was not long before I started flying first officer on the B-99, building the coveted multi-engine flight time the major airlines required. There were other female pilots at Colgan and we often flew together, particularly if we had an overnight trip, as pilots had to share a hotel room. While I continued to build my time as first officer, I took my Airline Transport Pilot (ATP) checkride, but was not old enough to get the certificate. So on my twenty-third birthday, I went to the FAA and received my earned ATP certificate. While the airlines had pilots on furlough in the late 1970s and early 1980s, I was building my time to be ready for the beginning of the next hiring spree, and timing was on my side.

Shortly after getting my commercial license, I applied to both United and American with a copy of my retirement letter, a gimmick that was my mother's idea to grab their attention. I figured it was worth a shot. Over the years, I would send them information seeking a pilot's job, and my files grew. As soon as American started hiring in 1984, I flew to DFW and walked into American Airlines, looking for job without an invitation for an interview. Pilot recruitment invited me back to talk, as they recognized my name as the applicant with the fat folder. They gave me official forms to fill out every 100 flight hours, and when I reached 1,000 hours multi-engine time, they would invite me back for a real interview. Sure enough, I got invited back for an official interview. The interview process included three different interview trips to American Airlines in Texas, which included a pilot recruitment interview, subject testing, psychological testing, a physical, a simulator ride, and, lastly, a captain's board interview. Although not legal, I was asked in the captain's interview if I planned to get married and have children. Answering while I had no immediate plans, flight attendants had the same schedule and managed families. They seemed satisfied with that answer, especially after they conferred with the captain whose wife was a flight attendant. I found out later that, because I was so young and projected to make captain at American Airlines very quickly, they were skeptical to hire such a young female pilot, not knowing how it would play out. With 3,500 total hours and 1,500 multi-engine time, in May of 1985, I was hired by American Airlines at 23 years old. I was the twenty-first female hired by the airline. As projected, I moved up the seniority list quickly. Timing was everything in regards to airline seniority.

When I finished my initial training as a flight engineer on the Boeing 727 in June 1985, my base assignment was Washington, DC, DCA. It was my first choice and it happened to be a junior base, so I continued to live with my parents in Vienna, VA. In December 1986, Terry Clairidge, another female pilot at the base, was to join our family for Christmas dinner. As Christmas approached, Beverley Bass became American Airline's first female captain, and her temporary first base assignment was DCA. Beverley was sitting reserve, on call, at a hotel, and my parents extended the Christmas dinner invitation to her as well. Christmas 1986, my mother, father, brother, Terry, Beverley, and I were sitting at the dinner table when it dawned on us that Beverley was a captain, Terry was a new first officer, and I was a flight engineer, all on the B-727. We realized how fun it would be to work together on the same flight, an all-female crew. We started planning! Beverley was projected to fly a two-day trip on December 29th. I had that very trip a day earlier, so I called the flight engineer on Christmas day and trip traded onto Beverley's trip. Terry was a new first office and had not flown in a while, so she called the flight office to "buy" the trip to maintain experience. The two-day trip started in Washington Reagan, DCA, and went through Dallas-Fort Worth, DFW, to layover in Oklahoma City, OKC, and back through Chicago, ORD, the next day. As luck would have it, Beverley was assigned the trip on reserve. The flight attendants were female as well, so it was to be American Airline's and any major carrier's first all-female crew. Three crew schedulers, based in DFW, flew to DCA that night to position themselves to be passengers on the historic flight the next day. They brought the crew red roses to wear in our lapels. My mother, father, and brother all flew on this historic flight as well. Word got to the press and they were waiting at DFW for the arrival of flight 417, DCA to DFW, December 29, 1986, American Airline's first all-female crew. Many assumed that the airline put this flight together, but it was done by the three of us at my parents' Christmas dinner table. As Terry humbly told the press, it could have been anyone, but she was just there at the right time.

A month later, I checked out as first officer on the B-737. Two years later, I switched to flying first officer on the McDonnell-Douglas, MD-80, and in 1991 at twenty-nine years old, I became American Airline's youngest female captain. Also in 1991, American lifted its nepotism clause and my brother, Greg Prior, was hired as a pilot. It started out as a good year.

But "Prior" times proved better than 1991. Within six months of being hired, my brother had a career-ending health event. Additionally, my father, retired from United Airlines, was diagnosed with lung cancer. Before his symptoms progressed, I wrote the airline's Vice President of Flight and requested jump seat authorization for my father to fly in the cockpit of one of my flights. I am very grateful for that opportunity, as it was a highlight moment for both me and dad. My mother flew on the flight, too.

As it turns out, I did get married and have a family. I met my husband, Chuck Welch, in college. We married in 1988. Five years later, the day of my father's funeral, I found out I was pregnant with our first child. We have been blessed with two wonderful, now adult children, Abby and Billy. My mother, after realizing she raised a daughter to believe she could have it all, stepped in to make it happen and became our babysitter. My career-family balance was made easy because of a very supportive mother and spouse. Thank you both.

My husband is now retired after a career as a high school teacher, administrator, and baseball coach. My mother is now our dog sitter. And after 32 years, I am still a pilot with American Airlines, still based in DCA, but now a captain on the B-737. If I am lucky enough to fly to age 65, I will retire with 42 years of service and be number one on the American Airlines pilot seniority list.

Thank you to the women who came before and blazed the way. And thank you to my past, current, and future fellow pilots. And most importantly, thank you to my family.

At four years old, my son was asked if he wanted to be a pilot. He responded, "No, that's a girl job."

My daughter decided to pursue flying and has earned her private pilot's certificate and instrument rating. The family tradition continues.

Tracy was hired as a second officer on the Boeing 727 by American Airlines in 1985. She is a captain on the Boeing 737, based in Washington D.C. Tracy enjoys riding her bicycle, playing bridge, and spending time with her family.

American Airlines' first female crew on December 29, 1986: Beverley Bass, Terry Quiejo, and Tracy Welch.

Best Layover Ever
by Jean Harper

The alarm jolted me awake at a painfully early hour on the wrong side of my body's time zone. Even for the 3rd of August, the starry sky of St. Louis was still deep black behind the hotel room curtains. My head and stomach ached as I showered and dressed in my United copilot uniform. Warm coffee helped a little. I greeted John, a cheerful, rotund gentleman who was one of my favorite captains.

While looking over the paperwork in flight operations, a wave of chill and nausea swept over me.

"Are you all right?" John asked. "You look kind of gray."

"I'm not sure. I woke up feeling a little yucky this morning."

"Yeah, this trip makes everyone sick. This god-awful early getup, a long sit-around in Denver—not long enough for a day room by *two minutes*—followed by twenty-four hours in Fresno, of all places, and all before noon! My copilots get 'sick' a lot, if you know what I mean."

Our stubby little Boeing 737-200 came slowly to life with the winding-up whine of the APU and the clank of solenoids. I got my second wind doing the walk-around in the sweet-smelling air. Admittedly, once I got past the pain, I actually liked being up before dawn. I guess I'd always be a crop duster's daughter at heart.

An hour later, we were climbing westward towards Denver with pale blue morning light at our backs. The flight attendant brought up hot breakfast crew meals, which we gladly accepted. Oddly enough, the appealing aroma suddenly made me feel queasy, like I'd flown one too many aerobatic maneuvers. What was the matter with me? I hadn't felt this way since....

I caught my breath. *Oh my goodness...* Could I possibly be...?

John chatted away happily between bites while I picked at my meal, and a short time later the sensation of mild airsickness disappeared as abruptly as it had started. It was my leg to fly, so I consciously dismissed all distracting thoughts and focused on planning the profile descent and approach. Our enlarging shadow rose to meet us as we touched down gently on Runway 26 Right at Denver Stapleton. John took the airplane at the high-speed turnoff and taxied us to the gate.

Inside flight operations, I made a discreet phone call to my obstetrician.

"So what are your plans for half the morning?" John asked.

"Oh, I think I'll run a quick errand," I hedged. "I'll be back by nine-thirty."

Forty minutes later I sat in the bright, slightly chilly doctor's office with my uniform sleeve rolled up to the epaulet and a tight rubber strip squeezing my arm.

"So, where are you off to today?" the nurse asked as she inserted the hypodermic needle and I tried not to flinch.

"Central California. I'm meeting a friend for lunch, another lady United pilot who lives near our layover city."

"That is *so* great!" she said with a bright smile. "I love to see women doing jobs like yours. Now, you already have a little girl, right?"

"Yes, Annie will be three this month."

She withdrew the needle, pressed on a bandage, and capped the dark red vial.

"Let's get you an answer so you can be on your way." She left, and I was alone with my thoughts.

United's pilot maternity policy was a flat prohibition from flying while pregnant, an addition to our flight ops manual that appeared the week we early female new-hires first arrived in January of 1978. Kathleen Wentworth, a United pilot who was also a lawyer, had been working diligently to get us a maternity policy comparable to what our flight attendants had. An agreement was imminent, but nothing had been settled yet.

The nurse reappeared, took a seat, and I held my breath.

"Mrs. Harper, your test is positive."

"So, that means, I *am*…?"

"Yes, it does."

An explosion of joy hit me like an ocean wave. The nurse congratulated me warmly, and I floated out of the clinic in a glow of euphoria. All the way back to Stapleton, I processed the miraculous news. What a life-changing, magnificent day this had turned out to be! I felt fantastic.

John had the papers ready when I rejoined him in flight operations.

"So, did you get all your stuff done?"

"Yes, I did," I said with a straight face. Slipping off my uniform jacket, I noticed the cotton ball and bandage in the crook of my arm. *Ooops*—I quickly peeled it off and dropped it in the trash.

"Well," he groused, "at least one of us had a productive morning. Let's put this trip out of its misery."

At pushback I snugged the seat belt and shoulder harnesses tenderly, and once again we were jetting westward on a glorious morning. Crossing low over Yosemite National Park and the foothills of the Sierras, we continued our descent towards the green and gold checkerboard expanse of the Central Valley. This was home to me. I was born and raised, and learned to fly, in a small agricultural town in the San Joaquin Valley not far to the north. In all my years of commercial flying, I never failed to get that pleasant heart-tug of welcoming familiarity every time my travels brought me to northern California.

At five hundred feet on final approach to Runway 30, I recalled with a smile landing on this very same piece of concrete eighteen years earlier, excited and alone in a Piper Cherokee 140, on my very first solo cross-country flight.

John suddenly bellowed.

Startled, I looked up to see bright bolts of electricity racing crazily back and forth across the windshield. He reached in front of my face, snapped off the window heat switches, then recaptured the glideslope with only the slightest bobble.

"Gosh, John, you were all over that!" I said as we exited the runway.

"Yeah, this happened to me before. Just to make sure we didn't forget anything, back me up with the Irregular procedure." I scanned the page from my handbook.

"Nope, you got it all."

Rounding the corner of the terminal, we were surprised by the sight of a shiny Stearman biplane parked on the ramp, its traditional blue and yellow military trainer colors gleaming in the sunlight.

"Wow!" we exclaimed in unison. My father had flown Stearmans in his crop dusting business in the 1950s, and I'd always been fond of those stocky, workmanlike airplanes. The thundering round-engine sound of my dad flying overhead was the beginning of my love affair with aviation.

"I feel so at home!" I exulted.

We parked on the tarmac while the airstairs were rolled up to the door.

"Isn't that your friend?" John asked. Waving from behind the chain-link fence was Molly Flanagan, a pretty, freckle-faced redhead, also a United 737 copilot.

"Go ahead," John said, "I'll take care of the maintenance write-up. This is going to shoot down the airplane."

I lugged my suitcase and flight bag down the metal steps and happily greeted Molly. In the ladies' room of the terminal, I peeled off my uniform and slipped into more comfortable clothes. I was quite hungry for lunch, as the morning's few bites of breakfast somewhere over Missouri had worn off a while ago.

"You can leave your luggage here," Molly suggested.

"Uh, aren't we going to your car?"

"No, we're flying to the Harris Ranch," she said, heading out the door towards the ramp. I followed, a bit confused. We turned the corner, and she strode directly towards that same beautiful Stearman John and I had admired while taxiing in! My knees almost buckled.

"That's *your* airplane?!"

"Yeah," she said matter-of-factly, and did a quick walk-around.

I stared in awe at the sturdy struts, brace wires, and stringers that ran, rib-like, underneath the fabric-covered fuselage. All my life I had wanted a ride in a Stearman, but dad's "one-holer" ag planes, reeking of sulfur and toxic chemicals, were not designed for passengers. "Stay back, kiddies," Dad would warn, "bad poison." He gently declined my childhood pleas to at least let me ride on his lap as he sprayed the fields.

This clean airplane, however, was no smelly crop duster—it had the intoxicating metal/avgas/dope-and-fabric aroma of a vintage flying machine.

"Climb on in," Molly said, directing me to the step and handhold for the front cockpit. I hefted myself up and settled into the deep, metal-sided cocoon while she fitted me with the leather helmet intercom.

A minute later, the metallic whine of the starter erupted into the irregular staccato of a big radial engine at idle. Molly taxied us out, got the takeoff clearance, and said, "Your airplane."

I was stunned! She knew I had Twin Beech and DC-3 experience, but this was her Stearman, an unfamiliar airplane with long, stiff legs. Still, I wasn't about to turn down such a generous offer. Peering through the miniature windscreen, I lined up on the centerline and pushed the throttle—a little too quickly, because the engine belched.

"Easy," Molly said kindly. *Darn it*, I scolded myself. I knew better. This time I advanced it gradually until the engine attained its full-throated, blatting roar. We drifted left, I corrected with too much rudder, and the airplane lurched. I could hear Molly chuckle. With my heart in my throat, I felt the tail rise—and we were off!

"About a two-hundred-degree heading," she called.

"Okay. Sorry about the lousy takeoff."

"Oh, I've seen worse," she laughed.

The warm buffeting of the air increased as my heart rate slowly returned to normal. I found myself grinning hugely. Here we were, motoring along at a thousand feet or so in an open-cockpit biplane, feeling every little change in air temperature and even humidity as we cruised over orchards and large rectangular fields of varying colors. Having worked six seasons as a flagger on my dad's ground crew, I could identify every crop and even smell the occasional mild, distinctive aromas that arose from the fields below. At last I was experiencing the joy my father knew.

"There it is, off to your left," Molly called, but all I could see was a ranch building and a few parked airplanes. Then I spotted it—a short, narrow brown strip paralleling the highway that looked more like a sidewalk than a runway. I edged towards a downwind leg, too high and fast, but Molly didn't say anything.

Please, please take it I silently implored, vainly attempting to reduce the airspeed while descending.

"Um, I should probably make the landing here," she said apologetically.

"Oh, please do!" I relinquished the stick and she rolled smartly into an assertive slip that pinned me against the left side of the fuselage. In short order we were straightening out on final, a little low and shallow it seemed to me, until I looked out at the double set of stubby wings and remembered... oh, yeah, Stearmans don't have flaps. The touchdown was smooth but positive, and we bumped gently over the gravelly surface to the tiedown area. After the propeller chugged to a stop, I unstrapped and climbed out, beaming and exhilarated. Next to the generic, faded Cessnas, her Stearman was—hands-down— the classiest and most eye-catching airplane on the ramp. I couldn't stop glancing back admiringly as we walked the short distance to the restaurant.

We were ordering lunch when something mentally tugged at me, like an unfinished thought. Suddenly the morning's revelation came rushing back—*the baby!* I was astounded. For the past few hours, ever since crossing the Yosemite Valley, I'd been so engaged in the operation of two significantly different airplanes that I had completely forgotten about my new little son or daughter.

Over iced teas and chicken salads, we caught up on our life news—our mutual enjoyment at being 737 copilots after years of flying "side-saddle" and being furloughed; my delight in becoming a mom and raising an inquisitive, playful little girl; Molly's hopes for marriage and a family of her own one day. How I longed to share my precious secret with her, but it would have to wait. My husband deserved to be the first to know.

Once we were strapped back into the airplane, Molly fired it up, gave me the stick and suggested a slightly different departure heading.

"Aren't we going back to FAT?"

"No, Chandler Field. You can do some touch-and-goes there. I think you'd feel more comfortable on a bigger runway."

I was charmed by her generosity and trust and excited to get another chance to fly. The takeoff wasn't as erratic as the first, and after another pleasant jaunt over farms and fields, we entered the pattern for Runway 32 at Fresno's uncontrolled general aviation airport. The longer, wider paved runway was a reassuring sight, but my big airplane habits didn't do me any favors. An embarrassing bounce to a go-around was followed by an excessively high and wide pattern, but Molly patiently let me figure it out with minimal coaching.

My first tight-fisted landing made the tires bark—reasonably under control, but not pretty. As we continued the circuits, I relaxed a little and allowed the airplane to communicate its desires—the sweet spot of pitch attitude for optimal climb performance, when to anticipate the power reduction, the best approach speed that felt solid and stable. With each gradual settling of tailwheel to pavement before the next power application, the Stearman felt less like a venerable relic from the past and more like a real airplane.

"Okay, let's head back to the big airport," Molly said. She thoughtfully gave me the entire last leg as well. In golden afternoon sunlight, we touched down with a low-pitched chirp on Runway 30, which now seemed like a ridiculously excessive amount of concrete.

As we taxied back to the terminal ramp, I saw a United 737 parked next to a tall scaffolding with orange-suited mechanics working on the windshield. I noticed the nose number, and it was the same airplane John and I had brought in that morning. I laughed in amazement. The past few hours had been so much fun that I'd completely forgotten I was on a layover!

"Yeah," Molly commented, "that one goes out first thing tomorrow on the early flight. It's a San Francisco trip I like to fly every chance I get."

We pivoted around and the engine sputtered to a stop. With ears ringing lightly, I gripped the leather cockpit edge padding and eased myself down to the warm tarmac. I thanked Molly with heartfelt gratitude and a strong hug, then stepped back to savor the last moments of our adventure. She brought the husky radial to life once more, and in an eardrum-vibrating crescendo of sound, levitated into the afternoon sky. As the double wings grew smaller in the distance, I placed my hands lovingly on my lower abdomen.

"Hi, little sweetie," I whispered. "You've just had your first ride in a light airplane, and it was a doozy!"

The Holiday Inn van was idling in the parking lot, so I grabbed my hat, flight bag, and suitcase from behind the United ticket counter, thanked the agent and made a run for it. At the hotel, I spotted my captain in the restaurant having an early dinner.

"Well, hi!" John said. "How was lunch with your friend?"

"Oh my gosh," I exclaimed, sliding into the booth seat across from him. "Let me tell you all about it!"

Sleeping in for as long as I wanted the next morning and awakening to chirping birds was absolute heaven. And when the mild nausea returned, I smiled gratefully while taking deep breaths, knowing everything was working exactly as it was supposed to. I would call my flight manager sometime in the next few days, assuming a second positive result.

On the flight home that afternoon, I recalled many memorable layovers that stood out over the years—snorkeling in Hawaii, the silent dance of northern lights in Alaska, Broadway plays in New York City, a Christmas Eve dinner theatre in Portland with the entire flight crew dressed to the nines, sea lions barking by the pier in Monterey, or any trip where I was joined by a friend or family member.

But of all these delightful layovers—and many more that would come later in my career—this was the one that rose to the top. On this undesirable pairing that pilots tried to avoid, two fond life wishes came true for me on a day overflowing with surprises.

I could hardly wait to get home and tell Victor.

Jean was hired by United Airlines in January, 1978 as a flight engineer on the Boeing 737. She retired in June of 2013 as captain on the Boeing 757/767. Jean enjoys flying the family airplane—a Champion Citabria, decorating cakes, and volunteering at a homeless shelter.

They Said It Couldn't Happen...
by Terri Donner

The flying bug bit me at age 16 when a coworker at McDonalds took me for a flight off a little grass strip. Lessons began and a Private certificate was earned at seventeen. As thoughts entered my mind about making aviation a career, key players in my life offered their opinions. My high school guidance counselor declared there was no chance of airline employment in the man's world. Some "friends" hoped my expensive, dangerous hobby would go away. In 1988, at my 10th high school reunion, a classmate delivered the blow that "with your vision," you'll never get hired by a major airline. So I decided to be content working on my ratings and moving along in a professional direction and see what developed.

I had married, started a family, logged 3200 hours, and had my ATP by 1989. A new airline was being born in my hometown of Louisville, Kentucky. My little boys were two and five and avid fans of the hot air balloons that frequently flew overhead, as well as the airplanes I flew at work. My good fortune landed me a seniority number at UPS as a flight engineer on the Boeing 727 at age 29. I wasn't sure how I was going to combine motherhood and jet-setting, but I was excited to give it a try.

My kids had attended Ninety-Nines meetings since they were a month old. My oldest son, Nick, was queried by an 80-year-old member when he was about four if he was going to be a pilot like his mom when he grew up. To which he replied, "No way, that's girl stuff." Baby Chase was denied a ride to a monthly Ninety-Nines meeting the day before he was born by a husband of a Ninety-Nines who did not want to risk ruining his new upholstery. In my defense, he did arrive 10 days early.

But my daughter Amelia declares that I "saved the best for last" when she arrived 16 months after I was hired at UPS. Shortly thereafter, I upgraded to first officer. The industry was really popping and I was released to the line as a brand-new Boeing 727 captain on my sixth anniversary at UPS. These were incredible times.

The kids liked to accompany me into Flight Ops on short errands for bid packets or Jeppesen revisions. On one such trip, Nick was greeted by a senior management captain and asked, "What are you going to be when you grow up?" Nick was quick to reply that he was going to "be a UPS pilot and fly my mom around so she didn't have to fly so hard." I had no idea he was watching me so closely. UPS had a well-known nepotism policy, and his chances were nil of employment as long as I was there. But I quickly motioned the manager to silence when he started to kill his dream. I got my little pilot away quickly.

Fast forward several years. Many hot air and fixed wing pilots in the family provided ample opportunity for my kids to crew and take flying lessons at a young age. All three of my kids soloed on their 14th birthdays. The boys got their private and commercial Lighter Than Air certificates on their 16th and 18th birthdays. Amelia, named for "you know who," amassed 30 lighter-than-air hours but decided all she was interested in was a frequent flyer card. A little known fact is that UPS flew passenger flights in their 727s for five years from 1996-2001. I started flying at UPS knowing I could never take my kids along on a flight, but that all changed and I took each one separately on a trip with me to Cancun or Nassau. That was a highlight of my career.

Nick was investigating aviation colleges and split his education between Embry-Riddle Aeronautical University in Daytona Beach and Oklahoma State University. He had his sights set on a major airline career and started out at ExpressJet three months after graduation. After seven years and no captain opportunity in sight, Nick started to look around for a different path to the majors. He realized the best route to interviews was occurring at Women in Aviation annual conferences, so Nick joined WAI and attended regularly for several years and even presented a session on hot air ballooning after he won the 2012 World Championship. Soon Nick joined the roster at Atlas Air. With his new 747-8 type rating, he was circling the globe without the hassle of passengers. Life was pretty exciting having mother and son doing the same thing for competitor airlines.

Our careers took parallel paths that were looking for convergence. UPS modified their fleet in 2007 and parked all the 727s in the desert. I chose the wide body A306 Airbus as my next ride. I loved the changes in my flight schedule. I was able to transition to mostly daytime flying in all of North America and Puerto Rico. There was an explosion in internet shopping and UPS needed more planes and pilots. The big announcement came that the nepotism policy was being dropped soon. There was only one thing lacking for Nick to apply to fly for

UPS, his dream job. The obstacle was 1,000 hours of Pilot in Command turbine time in his log book. After 15 months at Atlas, Nick scrambled to PSA, a regional company that was hiring captains directly into the left seat. It took two years to meet that PIC requirement.

The summer of 2017, Nick passed the psychological exam and simulator evaluation. He was offered a first officer position about five months later. That firm job offer could not come a moment too soon for Nick and me as we realized our dream of being able to fly for the same airline. On the first day of class February 12, 2018, the new first officers were offered a list of the available fleet types to choose by birthday seniority. Nick was the youngest in the class at age 33, so he had absolutely no choice but to embrace the last flight officer position that remained. As fate would have it, the Airbus was that choice. Nick and I would be on the same fleet and we would fly together very soon.

There are so many times in my life when I was told I would never be able to do something. My previous employer said I could flight instruct all that I wanted, but I would not fly charter. That was an important step to build the flight time I needed for the major airlines. Some well-sought legal advice changed my employer's mind and I was able to progress to Beechcraft Barons and King Airs. Soon the major airlines accepted pilots with corrected vision. I was fortunate to land a major airline job in my hometown. My son followed in my footsteps believing he would never wear the "Brown." He kept on working on the qualifications. Pretty soon Nick and I will take to the skies delivering UPS Cargo while occupying the best two seats on the plane! Never underestimate the power of a dream and keep on moving towards your goals! Realize your kids are always watching you. I'm trying to keep flying long enough for my grandchildren to realize what their "Gogo" does.

Terri was hired by UPS in 1989 as a flight engineer on the Boeing 727. She is now flying captain on the Airbus 300, based in Louisville, Kentucky. Terri loves ballroom dancing and riding her son's jump seat—he, too, flies for UPS on the A300.

Break a Leg
by Nancy Novaes

"**W**hat do you want to be when you grow up?" is a frequent question asked of a little girl. Back in the 1950s, some answers would provoke an indulgent smile and roll of adult eyes. Newspaper "Help Wanted" pages were still divided between "Help Wanted–Male" and "Help Wanted–Female." Teaching, nursing and secretarial jobs were what was available to "Females."

The fact that I was born and grew up in New York City gave me advantages I wouldn't have had elsewhere. I worked as a secretary in a downtown office two blocks from where the new World Trade Center was being built. As a scholarship college student working to pay for room and board, my answers to the question of "what to be" were seriously considered by people I respected who encouraged imagination.

However, becoming a pilot was nowhere on my personal radar. My first flight had been at the age of six when my mother took me and two sisters on an airplane ride on Staten Island (before the days of the Terminal Control Area, TCA) in a J-3 Piper Cub. My excitement was intense; I remember singing aloud the entire flight. There were no pilot role models or opportunities for a New York City kid, especially a girl. Besides, the Staten Island airports were closed when the TCA was established, shutting down every small airfield in or near New York City. I could only remember that flight as if I'd dreamed it.

The 1960s and early 1970s were decades that changed America and my generation forever. The Vietnam War was raging and young men were being called up to die in a war that made no sense to us. There was the Selma march and violence in the south as African Americans sought equality. A new women's movement meant that feminism suddenly had a name and a meaning. I was proud to embrace it then, as now, unreservedly.

Despite the social unrest, it was also hippie-happy party time for America's youth. The halcyon days of the Woodstock nation led to more than "peace and love." Many of us were sidetracked by the opportunities, good and bad, suddenly open to young people who had been brought up to expect only marriage and cooking. I tried a number of occupations and had my own succession of businesses. Then I went skydiving.

Two years into my brief acting career, I starred in a dinner theater comedy touring North Carolina and Oklahoma. I'd always loved acting and was good enough to land a few small acting jobs between business ventures. We cast members decided that since we only worked in the evening and had all day to ourselves, that we would each do something special, something we "always wanted to do." The rest of the cast went for scuba lessons. I went to the local airport.

In theater lingo, you never say "good luck" to an actor, as that is considered bad luck. Good wishes are expressed by the phrase, "Break a leg." I took it literally. After a morning's lesson on how to handle the parachute and execute a PLF (parachute landing fall), I took my first jumps. Jump one was spectacular. Jump two was even better. During jump three, the wind shifted and I found myself blowing toward the concrete. I toggled the 'chute to move to the grassy area. Too low at that point, I found myself plunging earthward. My landing was too hard and I could feel the crack in my ankle. That was the end of my acting job, and, as it turned out, my acting career.

I had been fascinated by what the pilots were doing as I huddled in the back of the airplane 'chuted up and ready. I decided it would be more fun to stay aloft. So, in between business ventures, instead of acting, I took flying lessons. I spent my weekends in Stormville, New York, a small town a short drive up the Hudson River. I earned my private certificate in 1973.

Consumed by my newly renewed joy of flight, I spent hundreds of my hard-earned dollars renting and flying small aircraft. In 1973, Emily Howell Warner was in the news as the first American woman hired by a U.S. airline. A month later, Bonnie Tiburzi made news as American Airlines' first woman pilot. Despite my personal experiences at the airport where I constantly had to prove myself, it looked as if things were loosening up for women in this sex-segregated industry. I decided that though I would probably never see the inside of an airline cockpit, I could still find opportunities in general aviation. But then the first fuel crisis hit.

Long gas lines and higher prices for fuel caused convulsions at all levels of the U.S. economy. Many private corporations could no longer afford a flight department. For every aspect of the economy, it was harder to make a living. Mostly self-employed, I too was struggling. Flying as a profession still seemed like a long shot, even if I could have afforded the rentals and further education. In 1978, the second fuel crisis hit, worse than the first. For the aviation industry it was a disaster. Deregulation became law and airlines were furloughing, even failing. Pursuing a career as a pilot seemed less a possibility than ever.

Three businesses and one marriage later, in 1981, I resumed flying, earning my ratings and becoming a flight instructor and occasional charter pilot at Teterboro Airport just north of Newark in New Jersey. When I heard about pilot hiring at a small airline just up the Hudson from New York City, I rented a Cessna and flew myself up for an interview. I was the first woman hired by Command Airways (now Envoy Air).

The race was suddenly on in pilot hiring. Startup airlines were a new feature in the aviation economy. As a native New Yorker, I was pleased to be hired in 1985 as a first officer on the lipstick-red DC-9s of New York Air, as their second woman pilot. My career at the airlines had begun!

Nancy was hired in 1985 as a first officer for New York Air. Retired, she now enjoys sitting in the back of the plane sipping champagne en route to all the destinations she only briefly visited during her career. At home, she relishes digging in her garden in the summer months.

India's First Woman Jet Captain
by Saudamini Deshmukh

I was probably eight years old when I pointed to an airplane passing overhead and said that I was going to be a pilot when I grew up. My family tells me a story that a small, agricultural spraying airplane had come to our little town. The pilot was giving joy-rides for a price and I was the only one from my family who rushed ahead and went for a joy-ride.

After getting my Private Pilot License I had to stop flying, as we had no money. I joined a bank as an officer after my graduation. I became a member of the Indian Women Pilots' Association (IWPA) founded by Chanda Budhabhatti in 1967. I was one of the founding members of the India section of the Ninety-Nines, Inc., an international organization of women pilots based in the USA. In 1977, I had an opportunity to go to Los Angeles area in the USA and stay with and fly with the American women pilots, the 99s. Many individual 99s helped me during my stay of six months, as I completed 300 hours of flying and obtained the necessary licenses. My chief mentors were Wally Funk of the Mercury 13 fame, Margaret Callaway of San Pedro, California, and Norma Futterman of Beverly Hills, California. Those were memorable days, and it was a life changing experience for me. It was my first trip outside India, and it was mind boggling to see America and its people and their lifestyles. It was like going to another planet—going to the moon. I owe a huge debt of gratitude to the IWPA and the Ninety-Nines, Inc.

I was hired by Indian Airlines (IA) in 1980 to fly the Fokker Friendship F-27, a twin engine turbo-prop airplane. I became a captain on the F-27 on September 12, 1985.

I had a very interesting, fascinating, and challenging career. On the F-27 there was no voice recorder and no simulator. We used to do the six-month checkrides on the airplane itself with only the instructor/inspector onboard with three or four pilots. We used to do scores of take-offs and landings with two engines running or one engine switched off. We were based in Calcutta (now Kolkatta) and we used to fly to all the small airstrips in the northeast of India. Many runways were just 5,000 feet in length with no Instrument Landing System (ILS). Some did not even have a VOR but had only an NDB (ADF). There was an airfield called Teju where we were told that elephants roamed on the runway at night! We used to fly over the river Brahmaputra, the broadest river in India. We used to night stop in little towns which had tea plantations around them. The whole area is at the foot hills of the Himalayan Range, and the weather conditions are tough.

I moved on to the B-737 and shifted to Mumbai. Even on the B-737, we used to land on very short runways (5,000 feet +) without ILS and VOR by doing NDB (ADF) letdowns in bad weather conditions. The ATCs in India did not have radar coverage in those days. The modernization of Indian Airports and ATCs started in the mid-1990s. Now of course we have long runways with ILSs and ATC coverage everywhere.

I moved on to the A320 and retired on the A320 after flying it for almost twenty years. I had the training and experience of doing automatic landings in thick fog—quite a change from the days of ADF (NDB) letdowns. We used to fly the A320 to all the countries in the Gulf and to Bangkok and Singapore, apart from the whole of India.

During my Calcutta days I had an opportunity to fly Mother Teresa. I have also flown well known film stars, politicians, and sports persons.

I was fortunate to receive felicitations at the hands of the late Mr. J.R.D. Tata at the Bombay Flying Club. J.R.D. had founded Air India in 1932. It was a privately-owned company for a long time and came under government control later on.

I had many firsts in aviation to my credit, and my name was well known in India. Passengers used to love and remember my soft landings. I received a lot of love and affection and respect from my airline people and the people of my country, India.

Indian Airlines and Air India merged in 2007 and became one airline: Air India. Thus I joined Indian Airlines in 1980 and retired from Air India in 2010. I retired as the General Manager of the western region and had a grand last flight with ATC congratulating me all along and the Fire Brigade water shower on my airplane when we landed in Mumbai. One cannot ask for more.

Ours is a government airline. We retire at age 58 and then fly in the same airline as contract pilots until the age of 65. I retired at 58 and flew as a contract pilot for a couple of years and then stopped flying in July, 2012.

--Goodbye, Aviation--

Saudamini was hired by Indian Airlines in 1980. She retired July 12, 2012 from Air India. Saudamini loves listening to music and reading.

My Dream
by Aileen Watkins

My dream of forty-five years became reality on February 27, 2017, when I assumed command of "The Queen of the Skies" for Atlas Air. It has been an incredible journey of a million miles, a million smiles, and many experiences which color my logbook pages as I reflect on the decisions and turns in my airline career that I have enjoyed for over twenty years. Along the way, I have had my husband of twenty-six years, Bob, by my side. Sharing this accomplishment with him is a beautiful gift.

My operating experience flights were fun, challenging, enlightening, and a joyful experience working with Captain Julie Morris, Line Check Airman extraordinaire. We departed Anchorage, Alaska, for Incheon, South Korea on February 10, 2017—my first leg flying the left seat on the 747-8. A big thank you to my Anchorage friends for the great takeoff photo and some great video footage!

With flights to Singapore, Hong Kong, Narita, and more Incheon, I saw friends old and new along the way. During our stay in Hong Kong, we met up with dear friend and FedEx pilot, Wenyu Fu. We ran around Hong Kong and made over 21,000 steps with a full-day hike on Cheung Chau Island. I so love my job!

My line check consisted of a "pilot monitoring" leg from Hong Kong to Incheon, then a "pilot flying" leg to Anchorage. We started the day in tropical sunshine and ended with moderate snow. We planned on a CAT III landing, with the ANC ATIS calling for 1/4 mile in snow and OVC 001. After a full briefing and set up for the autoland, I had to laugh when, at 1,000 feet, we saw the haloed lights of Anchorage. After taxiing in, I could not wipe the smile off my face. We signed the paperwork, debriefed, and I felt overwhelmed with pride, happiness, and a true thankfulness for the support of my family, friends, and ISA. Many women have served as my inspiration, and the hundreds of women I have met through ISA have walked with me through my journey to this moment.

My first flight off IOE was with friend and fellow Long Islander, Eric Brauer. We flew N263SG, one of our SonAir birds, on a ferry flight from Miami to Houston's IAH, my home airport. My husband, Bob, has been an Airport Operations Supervisor for IAH for almost twenty years.

The flight was a repositioning for one of our Houston Express flights from IAH to Luanda, Angola, leaving later on that morning. We planned to arrive at 0530 local. Being empty, we made it from sea level to FL400 in thirteen minutes! On arrival, we broke out around 1,000 feet and I could see the airport operations vehicle on the taxiway adjacent Runway 27. Upon landing, we received a congratulations from our female controller, then taxied in to Gate D12. While completing the logbook, my husband Bob, my beautiful daughters Alianne and

Katalin, and Captain Lynn Rippelmeyer (UAL/CAL retired) came up to the flight deck and gave me the biggest hugs EVER!

During my teenage years, I watched a television show about aviators on PBS and saw a woman—a CAPTAIN—preflighting a Continental 747. The vignette of approximately eight minutes changed my life forever. I had the opportunity to see a 747 very early in my life, and to see a woman airline captain in command sealed my fate; I knew what I wanted. My ultimate goal became 747 pilot. But how would I get there? A fantastic journey began, and now here I am.

Lynn and Sandra Stephens interviewed me for an ISA Scholarship in 1999. At the time, I did not know until the interview was complete that Captain Lynn Rippelmeyer, the woman sitting across from me, was the woman I had seen on television all those years ago. ISA had just given me the ULTIMATE gift. To have met my inspiration as a colleague, a peer, was the most incredible opportunity I could ever been given. Since that time, my focus and resolve were steadfast, and that airway (with several airlines along the way) led me to Atlas Air. Here, I fly the 747-400 (passenger, freighter, and VIP configuration), the Dreamlifter B747-400 LCF, B747-400BCF, and the new B747-8. I get my 747 fix every flight!

During my airline career, many ISA women supported me through advice given on the challenges of balancing career and family. After a ten-year struggle with infertility, my beautiful daughters Katalin and Alianne were born. I flew with both of them while pregnant and got heavily involved in research behind the issues associated with flying long haul while pregnant and postpartum. This led me into the advanced study of Human Factors/Aviation and Aerospace Safety, and a Master's degree and instructor position with Atlas Air focusing on Human Performance and CRM/TEM. My work with ISA as Human Performance Chair was an essential element of my studies. Today, I serve on our union Safety Committee at Atlas as the Human Performance and Safety Management Systems SME and chairman of the Critical Incident Response Program.

When my daughters were born, I had the opportunity to fly the Houston Express, which essentially was flying out of my base, IAH, to and from Luanda, Angola (LAD). This consists of a fourteen-hour flight to LAD, fourteen hours on the ground at the hotel, then about fifteen hours return. I did this once a week, three times a month, for ninety hours of pay credit and six nights away from home. It was the ultimate arrangement. I flew this for over six years, with a few other fun months when I could not hold the Houston Express lines, and it was a phenomenal opportunity to balance family and career. It sure beats commuting to London, Stansted!

I had the ability to hold captain several years ago, but my choice to stay as a senior first officer was a gift that I was not willing to give up. In the last six months, changes in flights and scheduling left me with a decision to make, and with the support of Bob, Kat, and Ali, I took the upgrade. The timing was right, and we are making it work.

My ISA sisters, you are a huge part of this accomplishment for me, and I am forever grateful to you for your support, encouragement and sisterhood that is ISA. Thank you from the bottom of my heart!

Blue skies and tailwinds, my friends.

Aileen flew for Alaska and United Airlines before being hired by Atlas Air in June 2004, fulfilling her dream of flying captain on the Boeing 747. Aileen enjoys playing the bass, drums, water sports, being outdoors, and exploring our planet with her family.

Aileen Watkins with Lynn Rippelmeyer

Aviation is a Lifestyle
by Gayl Angela Masson

T his is the story of my life as an aviator. Aviation is a wake-up-until-you-go-to-sleep kind of deal. It consumes you.

When you fly or perform any aviation-related skill, you need to be alert and agile because you are responsible for lives. Therefore, it's important to take care of your health. The thing is, it's impossible to always be healthy—even in the best of times.

As an aviator, your feeding times may vary, which can certainly affect your health. If you tend to fly around the world frequently, your circadian rhythms and cycles may dance. As a pilot, you will inevitably end up somewhere else, quite probably in another time zone, so it is most convenient if you can keep your eating options open. The problem is that this may limit your nutritional choices. Health can be a tricky thing as an aviator.

An aviation lifestyle doesn't just influence your health. It also concerns your mind. You need to have a lot of knowledge, not just of how to fly but of all things aviation. For example, an aviator of any level—pilot, mechanic, dispatcher—needs to know their airplane(s). In fact, you may need to intimately know more than one airplane if you fly several types. Your airplane has an individual physicality, a replete set of mechanical parts that harmoniously hum a tune you need to recognize. And they have a religiosity about them. The hydraulic clank of the gear, the spinning of the trim wheel, the squeal of the tires on the pavement: a veritable orchestra of instruments. Recognizing these things is part of the aviation lifestyle. One airplane might like to land flat, one might like to flare higher, one might need more speed at touchdown. You develop a touch, a second sense, a feeling for these boney, sinewy creatures. Guide them carefully—with love!—and they will love you back.

The aviation lifestyle also has an impact upon your relationships. Friends and family may reorganize celebrations so that you can attend, such as having Christmas on the 28th or on New Year's Eve instead. Perhaps birthdays will be moved. When you fully embrace the aviation lifestyle, you have to understand that you might miss these and other important events. This is what is especially difficult. You might miss your only child's first step, the school play, a wedding anniversary, or the death of your father, because you may be in Bolivia, Moscow, or over the Pacific Ocean.

There are, you see, always trade-offs. But although there are many difficult aspects to the aviation lifestyle, there are also amazing adventures that go along with it. These occasions— these rare opportunities of a lifetime—work to counteract all the hard parts of the aviation lifestyle.

For example, you might fly past a meteor greeting the Earth not so many miles away or witness the dawn explosion of a volcano. You might be barricaded in your hotel during a military coup in Lima. You might marvel at tossed tear-gas reaching passers-by in Argentina or have to swerve to avoid a sandstorm of the great white sands of Alamogordo. Maybe you'll breathe in the aroma of spans of untouched red-beaches in Australia. Yes, as an aviator, you will discover sights, sounds, and smells no internet search can predict, replicate, or even begin to describe. It is this that is the most amazing part of the aviation lifestyle.

Angela was hired by American Airlines in 1976 as a flight engineer on the Boeing 707. She retired in 2007 as captain on the Boeing 777. Angela teaches flight at Embry-Riddle and loves traveling with her daughter, a meteorologist.

About Us

The International Society of Women Airline Pilots began in 1978 when 21 female pilots met in Las Vegas, Nevada.

Forty years later, ISA+21 is 500 female pilots strong. Our annual conferences are held around the world and are met with great enthusiasm. They are "energizing," one attendee said, and a wonderful way to renew and re-ignite old friendships and make new ones.

ISA+21 has also awarded over 1.3 million dollars in scholarships to over 200 women whose career goal is to be an airline pilot.

ISA+21 women in Las Vegas in 1978.

ISA women in Las Vegas in 2018.
(Photo by Desert Rose Photography)

Made in the
USA
Monee, IL